Joe Yazbeck

No Fear
Speaking

Praise for *No Fear Speaking*

"Forty years ago I received a book titled *Tongue and Quill* in the processing line of the US Air Force Academy. We were told anything we needed to know about effective communication was between its covers. It remains the definitive reference for USAF officers today. Loaded with wit, humor, and insight, *No Fear Speaking* challenges T&Q as the ultimate guide for speakers struggling to master the art of reaching an audience."

—David J. Scott, Major General (ret), USAF

"*No Fear Speaking* is a rare work on public speaking that is both readable and immediately useful. Yazbeck guides the reader, step by step, through the mechanics and dynamics of public speaking with clear, lean descriptions that not only convey the methodology but also the underlying logic with great insight. As someone who has worked in the high technology industry for over thirty years, this book taught me that public speaking and technical presentation is not an ancillary activity but a major essential to one's success."

—Gary Iosbaker, Distinguished Technologist,
CTO Telecom-Americas, Hewlett-Packard

"Joe Yazbeck's book *No Fear Speaking* is essential for anyone who wants to deliver effective speeches. It is a road map to success. Yazbeck's experience as a master speaker comes through with his multiple lists of what to do and what not to do, and his constant reminders of preparation and practice are the hallmarks of great speech making. Follow his formula and you will present great speeches!"

—Bill Lenahan, CEO, OffSite Vision Holdings, Inc.
(former CEO, Cingular & Bell South Wireless)

"In *No Fear Speaking*, Yazbeck's easy-to-comprehend approach is both thorough yet laid-back. He offers tips that truly benefit us rather than batter us round the head to drill the message home. His tips are pure gold. I'm a great believer in people who talk the talk having walked the walk. If you're speaking to staff or to companies, motivating teams, or presenting to your peers, being able to stand up there, get noticed, and influence people will benefit you enormously. Yazbeck is the real deal: he is a great speaker on and offstage—and now he is showing you how to be one!"

—Tony Michaelides, former record promoter and publicist
for U2, David Bowie, Whitney Houston, Peter Gabriel,
Bob Marley, Genesis, The Police, Annie Lennox

"Every once in a very long while we come across works that redefine a particular topic or subject. It took 40 years for the pendulum to swing and once again the world has found itself in a 'WE' time. Leadership skills have never been more important nor has the world ever been in greater need of influential, compelling and heart-centered leaders. In *No Fear Speaking*, Mr. Yazbeck makes it his mission to demystify what it takes to be a great speaker and leads the reader by the hand in the journey of becoming one. He is masterful at distilling the essence of what makes a speaker great. Nevertheless, his true genius lies in his capacity to communicate and educate through the book how to conquer the fear of public speaking, become an impactful communicator and ultimately become an influential leader. This book is truly a refreshing game changer! Thanks Joe!

—Mario E. Torres-Leon, MD

Co-Founder and President, The Thrive Doctors

Speaker, Author, TV Celebrity and Host of "Thrive Doctors Radio"

"If you are looking to become a great public speaker, read this book NOW. It contains the secrets of those who have naturally mastered the art of public speaking. Joe's thirty-year-plus experience in coaching all types of businesspeople, executives and artists, is entirely reflected in this amazing compilation. It takes away the fears and the considerations you might have while thinking about that speech you will need to produce and deliver to sell an idea, to solicit funds, or to plead for a good cause.

Having trained over 100,000 business owners and executives in more than thirty countries in the last twenty-five years, I did not realize I could still improve my speaking talent. That is, until I read this book. There is no theory here—just applicable, down-to-earth tips and techniques that guarantee to make you a professional speaker!"

—Patrick Valtin, Author, *No Fail Hiring*; CEO,

New Era Management International

"*No Fear Speaking* is a must-read for individuals and organizations. This book is indeed a complete confidence-builder. Joe Yazbeck's unique system will impact your ability to get your message delivered in the most professional and inspirational manner. Wisdom is the principal ingredient here!"

—Melvin A. Myer, President, CEO, Myer Financial Group

"The timid wallflower becomes the mouse that roars under Joe Yazbeck's experienced, guiding tutelage. The author's chapters embrace with clarity not only speech delivery, but also the vital off-air, off-stage preparations necessary for success at the podium. He concludes each with practical exercises that begin the reader's journey toward "no fear" speaking ability without delay. But that's only Part I. In Parts II and III, Yazbeck teaches how to 'perform' the scientific art of public speaking well beyond the level of scripted, monotonous presentations; to achieve the power to influence and inspire audiences with aplomb."

—Ronald Joseph Kule, Author, *Listen More Sell More* and *Chef Tell, The Biography of America's Pioneer TV Showman Chef.*

"Joe Yazbeck knows how to change ordinary speakers into dynamic speakers. In *No Fear Speaking*, he has shown how to help others reap the benefits of excellent communication skills in business and life."

—Neil Brickfield, Pinellas County Commissioner, Government Consultant

"Loved it! Smart, insightful, and totally useable, Joe Yazbeck's *No Fear Speaking* has all the ingredients for the beginner or experienced professional and everyone in between. *No Fear Speaking* will improve your potential to build your career and create lasting growth and income. Having experienced Yazbeck's very high-spirited and fun presentations, I can say that his personality really comes through in this informative and entertaining look at the important art of public speaking. As a professional who's spoken at more than 1,400 contracted events, I realized there were several areas that I could improve on. I came away feeling refreshed and ready to take my profession to the next level. This book is a MUST for your collection."

—Rick Rainbolt, Brand Expert, Speaker,
Author, Better Health Advocate

"In *No Fear Speaking*, Joe Yazbeck hits a home run. He presents a convincing and easy-to-follow process that, if adhered to, will result in a successful and enjoyable public speaking career."

—Lou Ramos, Colonel, USAF (Ret.)
Communications Commander, Desert Storm

"Joe Yazbeck is a force to be reckoned with, and that intensity comes through in *No Fear Speaking*. This very well organized book is a complete checklist for everything a person would need in order to become a 'No-Fear Speaker,' including instructions and drills for how anyone can successfully overcome their stage-fright. Despite being a celebrated author myself, I have had my share of hesitancy when it comes to public speaking. Reading this book has taught me the essential elements of *No Fear Speaking* and has given me a step-by-step blueprint of instructions for building those elements into a highly effective speaking experience. Whatever your speaking issues are, *No Fear Speaking* will help you develop the skills and confidence you need to be a successful public speaker, and will clear your path to becoming a master at it."

—Harry Frisch, author of *HOW TO SELL—Clear and Simple*

"A masterful book! Joe Yazbeck's *No Fear Speaking* has opened up the playing field for all of us to stand up and express our hearts and art and ideas. Truthfully, public speaking used to raise my anxiety level, on a scale from 1 to 10, to about a 42. Joe skillfully takes the mystery and the fear out of the process. So much so that public speaking is now joyful and fun."

—**Susan Pomeranz,** PhD, author of
Open Your Heart and Say Ahhh

"As an attorney with fifteen years of courtroom trial experience, I wish I could have read *No Fear Speaking* when I started my career. Yazbeck's book is an excellent resource for continued learning and improvement, providing sound practical advice while inspiring the reader. On the practical advice side, the book's lessons, checklists, and tips apply not only to speeches but to everyday interactions, from networking functions to boardroom meetings. How we speak and present ourselves influences how others will think of us and do business with us. On the inspiration side, the examples provided throughout the book and the call to action and compilation of quotes at the end are very motivational. I am excited that my new audiences will benefit from me having read this book and working through these exercises!

Just as Mr. Yazbeck inspired me through his book, I am now more able to inspire future audiences."

—**Kerry Raleigh Tipton,** Attorney

"Joe Yazbeck is an expert educator. I have personally witnessed him transforming students, frozen with fear, into competent speakers in just a few short classes. I am one of those students. His book, *No Fear Speaking*, is full of easy-to-understand wisdom. Read it, practice it, and then stand up and tell your own story!"

—Mark Lauter, CEO, Sumo Software Corporation

"Joe Yazbeck has written a wonderful book about the art and science of successful speaking and presentations. He gives us an easy formula and structure for measuring and evaluating successful speaking. This book is required reading for anyone who has to do public speaking. Public speaking is not a natural act, and thus the fear associated with it. *No Fear Speaking* reduces the fear by breaking down the event into observable and measurable activities which collectively make for confident, comfortable, no fear speaking. Thank you, Joe, for such a wonderful and timely book. You saved my life."

—Bruce Elliott, International Consultant, Franchisor, Entrepreneur

"I love this book! *No Fear Speaking* brings out your best and inspires you to challenge your own speaking abilities. Joe Yazbeck will help you enhance your image as an expert in your field. This book is a must-read for any professional speaker—from beginners who suffer from stage fright to seasoned professionals who would like to fine-tune their techniques."

—Bobbi Janson, Speaker, Author of *21 Steps for Success in the New Music Biz*

No Fear Speaking brought my public speaking skills to a new level. Before reading this book I had done plenty of presentations and considered myself a good speaker; however, Mr. Yazbeck's book taught me new skills that have honed my presentation abilities. I am now more confident than ever with my public speaking skills.

By the time you read the first third of the book, your ability to speak in front of an audience will have dramatically improved. This book is a must for people at all levels of public speaking skill.

—**Ken Lark,** Attorney

"In *No Fear Speaking,* Joe inspired me to work the presentation process backwards. I have always been a 'wing' kind of guy—light the audience and then see what happens. But now I realize through this book that knowing the outcome, purpose, and audience first helps me decide what I want to have happen at the end and then light the audience in that direction. He has made it simpler and easier to effectively speak to and influence any group."

—**Wayne Moritz,** CEO, RainMaker – RainSaver Corp / Warp7Software LLC

"From the knee-knocking, boot-shaking beginner to the seasoned pro, there's something to be learned by everyone. For me, *No Fear Speaking* captured some of the little things that mostly go unnoticed to less seasoned speakers and brought to light a couple of areas to focus on the next time I go 'live' speaking, coaching, or training. I appreciated the insights and the additional perspective that I gained by seeing into Yazbeck's methods and thinking processes as a real pro with hundreds of speeches under his belt. Most people get the 'big things'; Yazbeck captures the all-important 'little things.' He hasn't just put together a book to read, he's built a manual to be studied and practiced for life."

—**Russ Laggan,** Speaker, Trainer, Coach; CEO, Laggan Inc.

"Joe Yazbeck's *No Fear Speaking* is a call to action, a compelling call to own the space, the message, and, ultimately, the audience."

—Chris Paradies, Attorney, Paradies Law Group

"Words fail me . . . I'm speechless . . . Couldn't put it down . . . A must, fun read."

—Mike Marget, President, CEO, 4 L Law Cloud Services;
Former CFO, Holland & Knight Law Firm

"I've been reading self help books on sales and public speaking for over 40 years. I've been personally involved in these areas for even longer. I've presented to a single audience with as many as 5,000 people and mentored dozens. I've never seen a better plan for speaking effectively. Joe has a practical approach, logically organized, well articulated with sequentially organized tasks and checklists that are so simply explained that virtually anyone can do it. No Psychobabble, no Mumbo-jumbo, no vague generalities. Straightforward and clear, inspiring and motivational and results oriented. A MUST read for anyone involved in speaking EFFECTIVELY."

—Marshall Kornblatt, Exec. VP of a
Major International Insurance Co.

"I Liked the simplicity and the common sense approach to effective public speaking in this book. It provided valuable tips that I tried with recent groups that gave me an advantage in gaining the messages acceptance. IT HELPED MY SALES!"

—Frank Suarez, Owner Natural Health Facilities,

"I was very fortunate to be given a copy of Joe Yazbeck's *No Fear Speaking.* I have been a guest on hundreds of radio shows and dozens of television shows, and have spoken countless times to groups as large as 3,000 people. Having no fear of speaking, I wondered if this book would help. I was humbled and delighted to learn how Joe's powerfully simple instructions made me a more effective speaker. This book is invaluable to both the person with a fear of speaking and the accomplished speaker. You will not be disappointed, may be humbled, and will find your public speaking so much more improved."

—Steve Hayes, Attorney and Social Advocate

"This book was an outstanding read and great source to be able to give more effective and better prepare oneself to be a better public speaker. The chapters were easy to read and understand, and followed an easy flow pattern. I routinely speak on radio/television and at civic events and this book gave me added in-depth ways to better communicate with my audience. This book is perfect for corporate America, small business owners and anyone who just wants to be a better communicator. I was able to incorporate the various checklists and tips into my public speaking repertoire; it became especially useful when I had to give remarks at my retirement from the U.S. Marines. I would recommend this book to anyone who wants to be a better and more accomplished public speaker. Buy this book!

—John Ubaldi, 30-yr Marine Vet, Owner UbaldiReports.com

"How do you move people to action with your words? If you are in the business of selling anything, be it a product, a service, or an idea, you need to learn how to connect with and inspire your audience. Joe Yazbeck's amazing book will teach you, step by step, how to do it. From storytelling to audience involvement to speaking from your authentic self, Yazbeck reveals the essential ingredients that go into a successful presentation. Every person who needs to move a group or a prospective client into action needs to read this book now!

—**Dan Sherman,** Author, *Maximum Success with LinkedIn*

"Joe has created an exceptional guide with practical exercises that will enable you to begin immediately becoming a comfortable public speaker. This book addresses the key barrier to speaking in front of a group . . . emotion. While others discuss the mechanics of delivering a speech, Joe talks about the feeling of giving a speech . . . and the joy of doing so successfully. I will refer to this book prior to each of my speaking engagements to ensure I have all my bases covered!

—**Russ Barnes,** USAF Colonel (ret)
Senior Executive Toastmasters Int'l

"Joe Yazbeck is clearly a master of his craft. If you want to make a big impact in your market, speaking is where it happens. The simple and powerful presentation of this material is what you get in Joe's book. He gets to the heart of the matter without all the fluff. *No Fear Speaking* is a must-read book."

—**Sean I. Mitchell,** Author, Speaker, Media Consultant

Joe Yazbeck

No Fear
Speaking

High-Impact Public Speaking Secrets
to Inspire and Influence Any Audience

Published 2014

ISBN: 978-1-941102-00-8 hardcover

ISBN: 978-1-941102-01-5 paperback

Library of Congress Control Number: 2013957205

For information, address:

Prestige Leadership Advisors

2600 East Bay Dr Suite 230, Largo, Florida 33771

727-489-2349

Cover designs by Margie Rosenstein

Interior design by Tabitha Lahr

Front Cover Photo by Daniel Correa

Back Cover Photo by Wayne Cathel

Interior Photos by Lee Burgess and Ryan Gautier

Copy Edits by Ginger Marks

Literary Consultant, Norman Thalheimer

Contents

Part II: Speaker Magnetism

I dedicate this book to my phenomenal family: to my wife, Elisa; to my parents, George and Jane; to my son and daughter, Tony and Angela; and to my sisters, Donna, Joanne, Ceil, and Ann Marie.

I am eternally grateful for your undying, unconditional love and friendship and for the inspirational support you've given me throughout my entire life.

You all have made it so easy for me to open my heart and bare my soul, to speak fearlessly, and to inspire others to do the same!

Foreword

AS A STUDENT OF the art and science of public speaking, I have discovered that whenever we sit in an audience and listen to a speaker, we crave the answers to three questions:

1. Why should I listen to you? Have you done it, and are you currently doing it? This is the Credibility piece.
2. Can I do it too, with my limitations and my weaknesses and my strengths? This is the Hope piece.
3. How do I get from where I am to where I want to be? Will it be worth it to me? This is the Action piece.

If the speaker doesn't answer these questions, the attendees will not trust him or her, the presentation will lose its effectiveness, and the purpose of the meeting will be meaningless. And even if the speaker does answer these questions, if he or she engages us with only left-brain content, without providing inspirational right-brain illustrations, our up-close-and-personal time together is wasted. No one wants to experience "death by

PowerPoint"! In that case, the speaker might as well just email us the data and slides.

We don't learn to know; we learn to do. Knowledge is power, but knowledge has no heart. All the information in the world is not going to make a person successful. It's like the guy who has three PhDs: one in philosophy, one in psychology, one in sociology—he doesn't have a job, but at least he can explain why.

This is why we have meetings! This is why there is value in getting together for a heart-to-heart, belly-to-belly conversation! When it comes to being a powerful speaker, reason leads to conclusions, but it is emotion that leads to action.

For these reasons, it is my privilege to introduce to you my friend Joe Yazbeck, who has more than thirty years of experience as one of America's foremost executive leadership trainers and presentation/ performance coaches. Trust me when I say you should listen to him.

Although this book is not long, its content is comprehensive, as every page delivers part of Joe's famous formula for elegant eloquence, edited down so that every word "pays its own way". With an easy-to-understand, practical recipe that everyone can implement immediately, not only will it help you realize you can do this, too, but when you click off your reading light at the end of the final page, you will know exactly "how to get from where you are to where you want to be, and that yes, being an awesome speaker will definitely be worth every effort."

Personally, I love Joe's precise advice, including:

- Clear and concise instructions on how to organize a great speech

- Detailed direction on how to write a compelling introduction and a memorable close

- Curious questions to customize your content

- Terrific tools to engage and inspire the audience

- Help with where and when to add humor

- Compelling ways to call for action

Bottom line: Yes, you should hire Joe to be your personal speaking coach. Yes, you should attend his seminars. But until you can and do, this book will lead and guide you, stand beside you, and help you master more meaningful corporate communications, exponentially improve every sales presentation, and guarantee that you will deliver a well-organized, emotionally choreographed, powerful presentation every time you are invited to speak.

—Dan Clark, CSP, CPAE

New York Times best-selling author, CPAE Hall of Fame speaker, screenwriter, gold record–winning songwriter and recording artist, adventurer, journalist, university professor, international consultant, philanthropist

Dan Clark serves on the International Board of Governors of Operation Smile and on the National Advisory Board for Operation Kids. He is an award-winning athlete who fought his way back from a paralyzing injury that cut short his NFL football career, whose incredible bucket-list included his U2 Space Flight.

www.danclarkspeak.com

Preface

IMAGINE YOURSELF SITTING in an auditorium, or even a stadium, next to hundreds—maybe thousands—of total strangers. Suddenly you're called on by a voice in the distance to stand up before them and deliver the speech of your life. What would it mean to you to do this? Would the very prospect fill you with a sense of excitement and purpose—make you feel eager to reach the podium and sway the multitudes with your thoughts, observations, and most deeply held convictions? Or would it fill you with numbing anxiety, outright panic, and the sudden, overpowering desire to run like a gazelle to the nearest exit?

If you chose the latter answer, you're not alone. Most people cite public speaking as the number one fear in their lives—even greater than death! But here's another thought: Imagine that you were once truly afraid of standing and speaking before a packed crowd, but now you take absolute delight in it. You understand that you are doing the very thing most people in the audience are too overwhelmed to do. You also understand that you have in your very hands the power not only to shape your own life but also to inspire and move untold others through your courage, the artistry of your speech, and the measure of your words.

What would this mean to your life? You would be acknowledged as a leader in your field—honored, admired, held in the highest regard—and the words that you uttered about the subject of your choosing would be seen not as mere trifles but as something to be taken very seriously by those whom you respect. Could the world hold anything back from you if you were such an individual?

Masterful public speaking holds the key to success in your life. I would go even further, in fact, and say that it is the difference between life living you and you living a most extraordinary life. The life you've always secretly wanted to live but somehow never could. The life you know in your heart and soul that you deserve to live.

What's even more amazing is that becoming a first-rate public speaker can enrich not only you and your family, but countless others who may need the wisdom and knowledge that you alone have inside you as desperately as they need oxygen.

This is the reason why I have written this book—so that each person who reads it can reach their highest potential and achieve what they once thought was "overwhelming," "unrealistic," "impossible," or "out of reach."

I congratulate you on taking the first step toward becoming who you were meant to be. Our fantastic journey will take you from where you are now to the summit of your dreams as a No Fear Speaker. So let's get started!

Introduction

EVERYTHING BEGINS WITH a seed, whether it's a tree, a human being, an idea, a desire, or an action. For me, the seed that grew into my pursuit of mastering public speaking was planted by two painful childhood realities: an innate shyness, and the oppression of being bullied at school. These are not uncommon experiences, of course, but such difficulties inevitably push one to make a choice: withdraw and hide, or take a path of confrontation.

My choice was to confront my obstacles, and in the moment when I drew that line in the proverbial sand, I began a trek that led me to face my naked fears. Over the years, I have challenged myself to stand before audiences as an actor; to acquire all the knowledge necessary in talent development, so I could nurture and expand the talents of other performers in the music industry; to delve as deeply as I could into the hearts, minds, and souls of those coming to me as a life coach, so I could guide them along the road to fulfillment; to work with others in mutually shared business ventures that would serve not only individual aspirations but communities at large; to teach, after a lifetime of experience and knowledge gathering, the intricacies of public speaking to those who cried out for that need; and finally, to share this knowledge with you.

Whether you're a business executive, a lawyer, a salesperson, a technologist, a teacher, or a community leader, the message that I want to impart to you is that *you* can learn what it takes to become a great speaker. Using the vital information and the Drills for Skill^{SM} of The No Fear Speaking System contained within this book, you can learn the art of stepping up to a podium and unleashing yourself full-force on any audience. Even thinking about doing this is exhilarating, to say the least—but before we begin, I want to pose some questions to you:

- What are your objectives in learning public speaking?

- What do you want to get out of this process?

- What are the obstacles or difficulties that you want to personally overcome?

Seeds of inspiration planted early in my life have had a significant influence on me as a performing artist and speaker.

When I was five years old I loved to listen to the rapid beats of fifties music. One song I loved in particular was "Little Darlin'" by The Diamonds. One day, when my home was filled with saddened relatives and family friends gathering for the funeral reception of a relative, my mother decided to pick me up and place me on the kitchen table so I could perform Little Darlin' for the group. I started to sing and within seconds the song had changed the mood and raised the spirits of the entire crowd. This experience made me decide that performing for others was a very positive activity.

I also have a vivid memory from the late fifties of watching, with my father on black-and-white TV, the great evangelist, Billy Graham, deliver a searing speech to tens of thousands of people in a stadium. At the tender age of seven, I was both impressed and astounded that one person could influence and command so much attention and respect from so many people. That experience made quite an impact on me.

Fast-forward twenty-five years, and there I am watching my three-year-old son, Tony, pointing to a TV in the next room, his small body swaying, and looking at me with a pleading expression. "Dad, can I do that? I really wanna do that!" I walk into the next room to see what he is pointing at on the television. It's Fred Astaire and Ginger Rogers dancing with dramatic flair in what I believe was the film Swing Time.

Here then, are my seeds of inspiration, influencing a new generation: my talented kids. Angela, my daughter, is a successful performing and recording artist, and Tony, my son—who landed his first role in a musical on Broadway (Gypsy with Tyne Daly) at the age of eleven (in 1991), is considered today's premier song and dance man on Broadway.

As the seed existed for me, it also does for you, and undoubtedly it's what has brought you here today. But for the words to come together, to register, and do their work of alchemically transforming you from what you were to what you will be, you alone must determine what your purpose is. Once you have defined to your own satisfaction what your objectives are and what obstacles you wish to surmount, you'll be ready to begin.

- Do you want to increase your opportunities to promote your product or service?

- Are you interested in reaching or attracting more people at once?

- As a business owner or executive, are you interested in exemplifying your leadership by appearing more confident in public?

- Are you eager to build your credibility and reputation for sincerity as a community leader or fundraiser?

Becoming a more dynamic presenter—a No Fear Speaker—will improve your potential for career success, growth, and increased income. So what are you waiting for?

You'll discover that this book is organized in a very simple, logical, and organic fashion. It consists of three sections: Speech Design, Speaker Magnetism, and Moving Your Audience.

Part I Speech Design deals with the essential elements needed to construct and craft a compelling speech.

Part II Speaker Magnetism concentrates on the elements needed to become a commanding speaker.

Part III Moving Your Audience delves into what it takes to move your audience toward your specific call to action.

When properly applied, such information has the power to raise your stage presence from *fearful* to *absolutely assured.* However, this will not occur through an act of the supernatural. The most pressing requirement you must meet as you work through this book is an unwavering dedication to your goals and ideals, along with continual practice of the drills listed herein. The fundamentals must be practiced—and then practiced again. Those who become masters of their craft do so because they have thoroughly committed themselves to the task at hand and to undertaking all that is necessary to achieve their goals. In short, there are no shortcuts. With that said, and with your goals defined, we begin now with the first part of *No Fear Speaking*: **Speech Design**.

Part I
Speech Design

Design: the plan, form, or structure of an object, work of art, decorative scheme, etc.

CHAPTER 1

Vital Steps to Effective Speech Preparation

IN ORDER TO SUCCESSFULLY prepare for a speech, you must answer at least three major preliminary questions. If you don't know the answers to these three questions, then you're at serious risk of not hitting your target—of creating a presentation that lacks the impact and outcome you're hoping for.

I like to refer to these questions collectively as the **APP**^{SM}. "A" is for "audience"—as in, "Who is my audience?" The first "P" is for "purpose"—as in, "What is my purpose?" And the last "P" is for "product"—as in, "What is my intended product?"

Let me define these further.

> **"A" is for "audience"**—Who am I presenting to?
>
> **"P" is for "purpose"**—Why am I here?
>
> **"P" is for "product"**—What is my intended outcome?

WHO IS MY AUDIENCE?

You've got to have some kind of evaluation or analysis of your audience before you go in. *What does this audience really want to know? What are they interested in learning? What are their needs? What are their wants? What is their median age? What is their gender, race, economic status, political affiliation, and even religious affiliation?*

I want you to understand that the answers to such questions can ensure that your compass is pointing in exactly the right direction long before you get up to that podium. Once you know *who* your audience is, you can better define *where* you want to take them—and you can position your presentation to make the maximum impact on the people whom you're addressing.

I firmly believe in doing a pre-presentation survey; it's a great way to find out a tremendous amount about your audience. So whenever I book an engagement, I ask the person who is contracting me to tell me what their understanding is of the audience that I'm going to be speaking to, and then I do some background research on that group. For example, let's say I'm invited to speak at a summit that an industry-specific magazine is hosting. All of the subscribers of this magazine are going to be there—which means my audience will be composed primarily of people with a vested interest in one particular industry. Before I speak, I want to learn as much as I can about this industry: what its problems are; what issues it's facing economically and business-wise; what its means of getting customers are; whether its customer base is growing or decreasing. These facts will help me to understand the *needs* of my audience, and to support those needs in my presentation.

Human beings tend to be motivated by two things: achieving pleasure or resisting pain. This is going to help you to know what you're dealing with up front—preferably before you even arrive onstage. Is this an audience that is more motivated about freedom *from* something or freedom *to do* something? Are they more interested in learning about how they can *save* money, for example, or how they can *make* money? Are they pleasure-seeking or pain-avoiding? These questions are best answered before you begin, so you will be fully prepared to address your specific audience—to address *their* specific needs—from the very beginning.

Great speakers understand their audience within the first couple of minutes of delivering a speech. With time, one learns to get an immediate sense of what emotion is resonating with the audience. From there, you may seek to match their emotional level and then, during the course of your speech, raise it. This takes practice, but it is something that can be learned—in fact, it's something that I teach through scenarios in my training sessions.

WHAT IS MY PURPOSE?

Now we get to the second letter of the equation, the first "P," which stands for "purpose." *What is my purpose? Am I presenting primarily to give information? Am I presenting to entertain? Am I presenting to create some kind of call to action? Am I persuading somebody to do something? Why am I here?*

Perhaps you're informing your audience—providing them with knowledge so they become educated on a subject, as though it were a briefing. Perhaps you're persuading them of something or even reassuring them in order to get them to buy into or commit to something—a product or a service or maybe even a fundraising activity. Or perhaps your purpose is pure entertainment, like a Friars Club roast or an awards banquet. The bottom line is, you've got to decide what the purpose is and tailor your speech accordingly.

WHAT IS MY INTENDED PRODUCT OR OUTCOME?

The final "P" in our formula stands for "product," and it's the element that gets neglected the most. I'm not talking about what you're selling; I'm talking about *what is the product of your presentation? What do you want the presentation to result in? What do you want it to move your audience toward? What is your call to action? In what way do you want that to happen? What instructions are you giving your audience so that you know they're receiving your intended product?*

Maybe your intended product is for your audience to make appointments with you for a later date. Maybe it's for them to go to your website and download a DVD or a book. Whatever it is, your product *needs* to be named. And you need to have that in mind so that you can write a concise statement about what both your purpose and your product are.

If you write and compose that statement at the top of your outline, then you know you will always be in alignment with your purpose and product. How you open your presentation will be in alignment with them; the points that you make will be in alignment with them; how you support your points in the body of your speech will be in alignment with them.

A product is what results from what you create during your presentation. How do you know that you have your product? Well, it shows up—in the number of appointments attendees make following your presentation, for example. Right there, you've got your product, and you can use the percentage of your audience who made an appointment to measure the quality of that product. Your numbers don't have to be astronomical, either—most speakers are content with single-digit conversion rates, in fact. The more you improve as a speaker, of course, the better your percentages will be. I've worked with speakers who double their conversion rates after undergoing training with me, and some who have even achieved 100 percent conversion rates at certain presentations.

NEXT STEPS: THE FIRST DRAFT

To ensure you've got the best possible ingredients going into your speech-preparation recipe, you'll have to take other steps besides thinking through the APP. For one, you need to do your research. Don't overload, but make sure you have sufficient material to support everything you want to say. If your presentation is based on what you know, then write down what you know—perhaps you can also gather some peripheral material to bolster it.

Next, construct an outline—the framework for your speech. Just as houses are built on cement and steel foundations and sculptures are built on armatures, a successful speech requires some skeletal structure to support itself. In order to build that structure, you must ask and answer the following questions: *How do you want to open? What will the body of your speech consist of in terms of the points you're making? How do you want to conclude?* The answers to these questions will give you the heart of your outline.

When you begin to think about the different parts of your speech, remember the following: you need to devise an opening that will catch your audience's attention; you need to have sufficient support for the points you're making, to build your credibility; and you need to craft a compelling, climactic conclusion—something that will move people to action. You'll also want to decide now whether you want to include a question-and-answer period at the end of your presentation.

All of these steps—researching your subject, figuring out your opening and closing remarks, deciding whether you want to do a Q&A—relate back to the APP. What you say and how you say it will be determined by your audience, by your purpose, and by your product.

EDIT, EDIT, EDIT

You're not done once you've written your first draft. In real estate it might be all about location, location, location—but preparing and organizing your presentation is all about **edit, edit, edit.** You'll have to cut the fat off the filet everywhere you can. You'll have to drill to get your timing down. You'll have to try out your presentation on camera and talk to that camera like you're talking to a person. You'll also have to write your own introduction. First and foremost, make sure it's laid out simply and that the person who calls on you can pronounce your name. That's no small thing.

THE CHECKLIST

As a final step in the process of preparing and organizing your presentation, you should make yourself a last-minute checklist. It will serve you much the way a pilot's checklist serves them before take-off. It's a safety measure. It will ensure that you have everything in order before you go onstage.

You should create your own special checklist for the specific event you're preparing for. Maybe you're doing a huge event on a platform stage. Maybe you're giving a presentation as a keynote speaker for a trade show association. Maybe you're giving a talk to a Rotary Club or facilitating a board of directors meeting or a stockholder presentation. Wherever you are, your needs will vary, and you should make sure you're ready to meet them.

Your checklist could include logistics, such as stage management, props, lights, sound, computer setup, etc., depending on where you are presenting. It should also consist of contingency plans. What happens if the lights go out? What will you do then? This may seem like an extreme example, but just look what happened at the 2013 Super Bowl in New Orleans. Lights go out. Power fails. Emergencies happen. I've given presentations in the dark before, with only the moonlight coming in through the outside windows to illuminate the room. For some people, this might have spelled the end of their evening; but it didn't stop me. To me, that's the difference between being a professional and being an amateur: a professional is always prepared for any eventuality.

In addition to your checklist, I would suggest that you have your outline on hand during your presentation. It's also helpful to create something I like to call "command cards"—index cards that you carry with you and that you can refer to, should you choose to, when you make your points. These cards shouldn't have a lot of content on them—just your main points. That way you can use them to prompt you if you need a reminder. I call them confidence cards because they help you maintain focus throughout your speech without fixating on your notes.

Let me finally mention in this section that while it's great to have your checklist, if you exhibit no spontaneity, your presentations are in danger of looking too "canned" and stiff. Remember, No Fear Speaking^{SM} is not only a science but also an art. Mastery requires preparation—but it also requires going with the moment.

THE BOTTOM LINE

In order to build a safe and secure house, you must first build a firm foundation. Likewise, building a successful presentation requires understanding APP and using that as the basis for everything that follows. Do you know who your audience is? What is the purpose of your speech? What is the result—or results—that you want to come from having given your presentation? You must be able to answer these questions decisively and thoroughly. Once you have, you will be able to construct a presentation that has meaning and substantiality and that will fulfill the objectives that you set for it.

EXERCISE #1: PUT APP INTO PRACTICE

With a specific, future presentation in mind, answer the following questions:

1. Who is your audience?
   (Answer in as much detail as possible.)

2. What is the purpose of the speech you are giving?

3. What results do you want to produce with your presentation?

CHAPTER 2

Speech Design: The Outline

YOUR PRESENTATION SHOULD feel unscripted and spontaneous. Devising an outline not only will help you prepare visually but also will serve as the cohesive framework for your content. The components of your outline—your *opening*, *body*, and *conclusion* (and *Q&A session*, potentially)—will become your organizational checklist, ensuring that your presentation includes both a purpose and a product that specifically target your audience.

At the end of this chapter, you'll find a **Sample Outline for a Fifteen- to Twenty-Minute Presentation.** After you have written your outline, you can transfer information that needs to be stated precisely onto what I call **command cards.** For example, instead of trying to commit to memory numbers or a quotation, you can look down at your command card and then quickly up, without breaking communication with your audience. What I say is: **don't memorize, recognize.** It's important not to fixate on your notes, but having cards with key points and information on

> ## DON'T MEMORIZE, *RECOGNIZE*
>
> Memorizing pins you to a script and interrupts what should be a continuous outward focus on your audience. Training yourself to use an outline or command cards with only the next key word of the major point of your presentation on them will prompt you to speak without sounding scripted and allow you to keep your attention where it belongs: on your audience.

them will allow you to appear natural and spontaneous without having to memorize everything.

THE OPENING

As you will see in the following outline, your presentation should begin with a strong opening statement that will gain attention and interest (more detail about this in **Attention-Getting Openings** in chapter 4). This is your opportunity to let your audience know they're in good hands and that what you're saying will be valuable. In other words, you need to tell them what's in it for them.

THE BODY

The body of your presentation should reveal the details of your message and provide supportive materials to back up your opening information. This is where you build your case by citing reasons for, and eliminating arguments against, your purpose (more detail about this in **Building Credibility within the Body of Your Speech** in chapter 5). Filling in your outline with supports will allow you to identify and correct any weaknesses in your presentation ahead of time.

THE CONCLUSION

Just as you must begin your presentation with strength, you want to end it with an impact as well. Your final words, and the emotion you express as you deliver them, should let the audience know what their call to action is. They have allowed you to be their "leader" for twenty minutes now, and you need to give them clear instructions as to what you want them to go out and do. You also need to be compelling and inspirational as you deliver your final message—so much so that your audience will not only remember what you have said but also tell others about it.

THE BOTTOM LINE

A well-crafted work of any kind starts with a clearly designed and thought-out structure. Before you can create a masterpiece, you need the framework upon which to build it.

EXERCISE #2: BUILD AN OUTLINE

Applying the advice set forth in this chapter—and referring to the sample outline on the following page—construct an outline with all three parts of your speech (four, if you're including a Q&A session) clearly demarcated.

SAMPLE OUTLINE FOR A FIFTEEN- TO TWENTY-MINUTE PRESENTATION

1. Opening

- Thank-you remarks and acknowledgments
- Attention-getting introductory statements or visuals
- Dissolving pre-conclusions of your audience

2. Main Body

- Major point one
  - Support sources for point one
- Major point two
  - Support sources for point two
- Major point three
  - Support sources for point three

3. Q&A period (if including)

4. Closing

- Call to action
- Final remarks

CHAPTER 3

Giving and Receiving A Great Introduction

THERE ARE SEVERAL DIFFERENT kinds of introductions that you may be called upon to make as a speaker. Examples of these varied introduction types include introducing someone informally in a meeting (perhaps the person speaking after you) as a way of granting them a position of importance; introducing someone out of an audience—having them stand up and affirming their value by thanking them or mentioning their merits; and introducing a keynote speaker (in cases like these, I like to make sure that I have a written introduction from the speaker—including correct pronunciations of names and/or words—beforehand).

PLAY YOUR ROLE

A vital point to keep in mind when you introduce someone is that you shouldn't "upstage" them—which, in theater parlance, means crossing in front of someone. If I'm introducing a speaker who is on my right, I want to exit left. If they're on my left, I want to exit right. Even if I wait for them to come to the podium and shake their hand before exiting, I should still **walk away in the direction opposite the one from which they entered.** That's key.

Say you're at a sit-down dinner with a tabletop podium at the front of the room, and you're the moderator. There is some stage management that must be taken into consideration in a situation like this. If someone is speaking while sitting down, you should remain standing, but you shouldn't make noise or move while they're speaking, or you'll risk taking attention away from them. If they're coming up to the podium to speak, however, you should shake their hand and sit back down while they have the focus of the audience, then stand up, shake their hand, and resume control of the podium when they're done. You have to think about vocal quality and proper sequencing of things, and you also need to have an understanding of what kind of event it is (whether it's formal or informal). All of these factors will come into play when you're making introductions.

WARMING UP THE AUDIENCE

When introducing anyone, particularly in a keynote or major part of a presentation, you always want to be sure that your inflection goes up, not down, at the end. Think of it as a sort of verbal drumroll: "Ladies and gentlemen, *Jim Smith*," or "Let's give a warm welcome to *Jim Smith*." A flatly delivered "Ladies and gentleman, Jim Smith" will be much less climactic. I'm not saying that you have to do a "Heeere's *Johnny!*"—but stirring the audience *is* an

EXAMPLE OF A HIGHLY DESIRABLE INTRODUCTION

Here's an example of an introduction that does everything right:

For more than thirty years, Jennifer L. Brubaker has been a community and business leader with a concentration on sales, marketing, and professional writing. She recently added an exciting new chapter to her career by establishing a nonprofit organization called the Women's Business Benefits Foundation. The foundation allows businesswomen to have a variety of benefits, including affordable health insurance. You will hear more about this from Jennifer in just a few minutes.

Jennifer is a business teacher at the University of South Florida in Tampa and holds a bachelor's degree in communications from the University of Illinois at Urbana-Champaign, as well as a BA in English and creative writing from the University of South Florida. In order to keep life from kicking her in the pants, Jennifer has earned three belts in tae kwon do and loves to challenge other martial artists. She also enjoys gardening and often spends her downtime curled up with a good book and her cat, Oliver. Please join me in welcoming Jennifer L Brubaker.

important function of anyone whose job it is to introduce others, and the way you do it is just as important as what you say. Just as a tasty appetizer prepares people for a great meal, a carefully planned introduction can whet the appetite of the audience before a speaker comes to the podium.

An introduction should not include the details of the speech to come, but it should list a few of the speaker's accomplishments and perhaps some interesting personal information about that person. You want to set the mood by "warming up" the audience with remarks chosen to highlight the speaker's credibility and spark listeners' curiosity about what they're going to say. A written introduction provided by the speaker is best. Please note that it is the speaker's responsibility to make sure that the MC delivers the introduction properly, with correct pronunciation.

Timing and physical presentation are also crucial. First impressions are made before you go up to the podium, so if you're the speaker being introduced, be aware of any mannerisms that might attract the audience's attention in a negative way, and pay attention to your cues.

THE INTRODUCTION: ESSENTIAL INGREDIENTS

- The Speaker's name, title, present company name

- The Speaker's noteworthy past and present accomplishments

- The Speaker's Key Affiliations

- A very short story, quote or description of the speaker that adds a personal, lighthearted touch of sincerity, humor, passion and credibility just prior to the announcement

- A professional, friendly, inspired and confident introducer setting a highly spirited tone for the audience

THE BOTTOM LINE

A cheerful, expressive, carefully edited, and articulately delivered introduction really sets the table for the featured speaker's opening to be well received. The importance of a great introduction is not to be underestimated.

EXERCISE #3: WRITE AN INTRODUCTION

Utilizing the tools covered in this chapter, write out an introduction that someone might use to present you to an audience. Remember, you want to both call attention to your own credibility as a speaker and hook your audience.

CHAPTER 4

Attention-Getting Openings

I'M SURE YOU'VE SEEN IT BEFORE—the most common approach to beginning a presentation is to start out with a quote or a joke. Unfortunately, unless you know exactly what kind of audience you're dealing with, this kind of beginning may come off as extremely contrived—and it may also completely miss the mark.

I can't emphasize this enough: *your opening should be appropriate to your audience, to your purpose, and to your product, and it should* definitely *get attention*. The truth is, even after your audience comes in through the door, in a lot of cases they still aren't quite "there" yet. They're still on the highway, yelling at the driver who just cut them off; they're still at the office, trying to meet a deadline; or they're planning their next meal. Essentially, their bodies are there but their minds haven't quite arrived yet.

So, how do you make an audience that isn't quite there listen with rapt attention to what you have to say?

TECHNIQUES FOR GETTING YOUR AUDIENCE'S ATTENTION

I like to get people to look at things in a different way, so I often start out a presentation by saying **something that will startle my audience**—something having to do with a current event, perhaps, or maybe a surprising statistic.

Projecting **visuals that provoke an emotional response** can also be extremely effective. So can opening your presentation with "You're not going to believe what happened to me on the way over here!" This kind of teaser has the potential to get people sitting on the edge of their seats, wanting to find out what unbelievable story you're about to tell.

You can also **ask a rhetorical question** that will compel the audience to really think about your remark. I call these **did-you-know questions:** "What in the world are they thinking of in Washington, DC?" "What are these boys on?" They're questions designed not to get you answers, but to elicit strong reactions.

Many times I favor opening with **audience compliments** because they can help establish a relationship right off the bat. If you can do this in a sincere way—if it's not forced—it generates a kind of love-fest, a mutual admiration society. It tells the audience, *Hey, we're all friends here—there's nothing to be worried about. This is going to be great for you.*

Certainly, **a story** is a good way to open as well. "Before I begin, I'm going to tell you a story about something that happened to me about ten years ago regarding a dramatic conclusion to a very hot business issue." Right away, you're sitting your audience in your lap and promising to take them on a journey. You're waking up their senses—their hearing, their sight, their smell, their touch, their taste—and, most important, their imagination.

You can **bring up a book** that you just read if it's relevant—refer to an author who had something important or weighty to say about the subject you're speaking about.

It can be okay to open with a **quote** or a **joke,** but only if it is appropriate to the situation.

I happen to also like **challenging my audience.** It's a very effective means of getting attention. For example, you could say, "By the end of this presentation today, I challenge you to take action on something that has not been given its due yet, and it's this. . . . " When you do this, you're moving your audience in the direction of *doing something.* (And at the end of your presentation, you could bookend your speech by saying, "If you recall, at the beginning of this presentation I challenged you—how close are we, ladies and gentlemen") This technique works very well at fundraising events and other events where you're trying to get people on board to do something.

AN OPENING WITH AN IMPACT

Here's another example I have from one of my clients, who was trying to find the perfect visual to set up her speech. This woman was about to give a presentation on weight loss and had opened up her own company after having lost 115 pounds in the past year. She decided to begin her presentation by bringing in a pair of shorts that she had worn a year before; they were about three or four feet wide—way too big for her new, slimmer frame. She held up those shorts and said, "These shorts were tight on me a year ago." Then she said, "My life has changed since." Now, *that's* a great way to open up a presentation.

DISSOLVING THE FIXED IDEAS OR
PRE-CONCLUSIONS OF YOUR AUDIENCE

After an effectively delivered and attention-getting opening, I advise speakers to take an additional step to ensure that they truly have an audience that is attentive and prepared to receive the main body or remainder of the presentation.

What I am referring to here are audience attendees who have made up their mind prior to attending as to what you are going to cover and the approach you might be using. In other words, they have fixed opinions or pre-conclusions about you or your presentation before you even open your mouth to speak.

This is a barrier for a speaker and one that must be overcome or dissolved, at or just after the opening, to ensure that you have your audience looking correctly at what you are about to cover with them. Otherwise, they have blinders on, preventing them from observing for themselves what you are about to deliver.

You need to remove these blinders or pre-conclusions to make it possible for your audience to be fully prepared to look at the real content and intent of your speech.

I like to tell my audience what I am *not* going to cover, usually by saying something along the lines of: "You might be expecting a canned or typical presentation or approach on marketing today; you will not get that. Instead what I am about to deliver is unique and newly evaluated information based on proven new case studies." You want your attendees to be thinking to themselves, "Wow, what *is* he going to cover today?" This is an eye-opener and prevents fixed ideas.

Your function here is to dissolve these fixed or pre-conceived ideas so that you have an audience willing and ready to hear exactly what you are going to cover. Now you are ready to deliver the main body of your presentation or speech as you have now an audience with an open and ready-to-learn approach.

THE BOTTOM LINE

Whatever technique you use to do it, if you want your presentation to be successful, **you must first get your audience's attention.** Set the table so that you can prepare them for what's to come.

EXERCISE #4: WRITE AN OPENING

Using one or more of the methods covered in this chapter, write an attention-getting opening for your speech.

METHODS FOR GETTING YOUR AUDIENCE'S ATTENTION

- Compliments and acknowledgments

- Questions and rhetorical questions

- Startling remarks

- Surprising statistics

- Humor

- Visuals

- Personal stories

- Referencing an important figure

- Referencing current news or events

- Quotations

- Challenging the audience

- Illustrative comparisons

CHAPTER 5

Building Credibility Within the Body of Your Speech

WHEN YOU MAKE A POINT, major or minor, in the course of your speech, it's prudent to back it up with materials and sources that will give it credibility. Such support sources have the power to add authority to what you're saying—to give weight to the points that you're making. It's important to achieve a certain gravitas onstage, and the employment of these support sources can be a great help in this area.

TECHNIQUES FOR BUILDING YOUR CREDIBILITY

Let's say that during the course of your speech, you assert, "The environment today is in bad shape." Well, yeah, okay—but that's a very general point. What you want to do is drill down—using specifics—to add credibility to your statement. Instead of saying, "The environment is in bad shape," you might say, "The environment today is in bad shape compared with where it was thirty years ago; in fact, in a two-year study published in the June 2007 *Journal of Environmental Resources*, Dr. Irving Smith, a climatologist at Harvard University, found that . . . "

Now you've just given the point you made some credibility: you cited a study, who the author was, his academic affiliation, the name of the journal in which his study was published, *and* which issue of the journal it came out in. This is not dissimilar to a court of law, in which an attorney makes a point and then has to bolster his arguments by either producing some kind of substantiated documentation or getting somebody up on the witness stand to support his side of the case. The whole rationale behind this is that *reasonable doubt has to be dissolved*. The same goes for you in your presentation: you need to dissolve whatever reasonable doubt might creep into the minds of your audience by supporting the point you're making with solid evidence.

I always say to my students or clients after they assert something in a speech, "Well, that's an interesting point you're making . . . but the audience members are going to sit there and say to themselves, *Oh yeah? Prove it.*" You should *always* have this idea in the back of your mind when you make a point. *How can I prove that what I'm saying is true? How can I make sure my audience has no reason to doubt my words?*

Giving **examples** of what you're talking about lends credibility to your presentation, as does citing **facts, figures, and statistics.** Incorporating **visual aids that show statistical breakdowns over time, pie charts,** and **illustrations** (a picture is worth a thousand words) can all be enormously helpful in substantiating your points as well. Even **defining a word** can aid in clarification or in supporting your argument.

I happen to love the use of **stories** to give weight to points being made, because stories are examples of your personal experience—you were there and you went through it. When you can give this sort of firsthand account, your audience thinks, *Oh, he was there. He's defining exactly what he means by his own experience.*

Testimonials and **analogies,** used wisely, can also give weight to your words, while the usage of **historical background** can be an effective means of bridging time and supporting your position. "Ladies and gentleman, this has been proven true by history time and time again. I'll give you an example: back two hundred–some years ago . . . " It's also appropriate to **cite an authority** or use a **noteworthy quote** to show by reference that the point you're making is supported by something (or someone) of substance.

THE BOTTOM LINE

Credibility is one of the five commanding qualities—The **5 C's**^{SM}— you'll need to possess in order to be a successful public speaker. The 5 C's are covered in more detail in chapter 9. When you add caring, comfort, confidence, and charisma to this credibility factor, your audience will be sitting there saying, "I really trust this person." (We'll go into more depth about the 5 C's later, in part II.)

Once you've established your credibility along with the other commanding qualities, you've got yourself a full and complete performance—one that will make your audience move in the direction of your call to action.

EXERCISE #5: USE SUPPORT SOURCES

Write three major points that you plan to use in your speech, then come up with at least two support sources (as delineated in this chapter) for each one.

SUPPORT SOURCES THAT BUILD CREDIBILITY

- Facts, figures, and statistics

- Historical documentation

- Definitions

- Examples

- Illustrations, analogies, and comparison charts

- Anecdotes and personal stories

- Testimonials

- Authoritative references

- Noteworthy quotes

CHAPTER 6

Using Transitions to Keep Your Audience Interested

IN THE ORGANIZATION OF YOUR presentation, one thought should follow another as you move point-by-point, for it's the sequence of these thoughts and points that helps the audience stay with you from beginning to end. Similar in function to the sinews of the body, transitions are meant to tie together, to unify, to create a logical sense of wholeness. Without good transitions, your speech can come off as scattered and disjointed.

> **TRANSITION:** movement to a new point or section of your speech.

EXAMPLES OF GOOD TRANSITIONS

Effective, workable transitions can consist of any of the following examples:

- **Bridge words or connective phrases,** like "incidentally" and "by the way." These words and phrases keep your presentation moving along by allowing one thought to flow into another.

- **Prompters or triggers,** like "In case you were wondering" and "Speaking of." These phrases can be used to activate, generate, or prompt your next point.

- **Questions or rhetorical questions,** like "Would you like to know what I did next?" (direct) or "Will you believe what I did next?" (rhetorical). Rhetorical or not, questions keep the attention of the audience and provide a reason for their involvement.

- **Flashback phrases** that suddenly recall information, such as "All of a sudden, I realized" or "That reminds me of the time," make a presentation appear spontaneous and sincere.

- **Bullet points** announce to the audience at the beginning of your presentation that there is a specific number of things that you will be explaining; speaking them in order prepares your audience for what to expect and helps them follow along.

- **Audiovisual aids** that highlight and illustrate the specific points that you want to make. Flowing from one visual to another or using visuals to connect one verbal point to another is an effective transitional method. Make sure that these visuals are visible to all members of your audience and that you incorporate them smoothly into your presentation.

- **Meaningful pauses** after startling statements or statistical citations give your words emphasis and can be extremely powerful and effective. They let the audience know you have just said something important, and they build anticipation for your next words. You may also pause between points to let the information sink in, and to indicate to your audience that you're about to move on to the next point.

- **Physical movement,** such as moving forward to introduce a point you're making and then moving back when you've finished, or emphasizing your points with hand and arm movements, can be used to both visually impact your audience and create a smooth flow from one point to another. In physically moving your body from one location to another, you can literally show your audience that you're transitioning to a new point.

- **Humor or storytelling** doesn't just add levity to a presentation; it can connect your points to a story or an amusing thought that will carry you forward to your next point to be made.

- **Examples between points**—either testimonials or descriptions of personal experiences—can help to drive home and connect the points you're trying to make.

For instance, if you have a ten-point system for how to accomplish something, you might provide examples of each point, thereby avoiding a robotic or boring rundown of one to ten on a list and at the same time creating continuity between them.

THE BOTTOM LINE

When you craft a speech, you're constructing something that needs to be whole and organic, much like a piece of music or architecture. Form follows function—you don't want to distract your audience from your message by causing them to focus on something that you consider to be immaterial. Using the transitions cited above will help you to create a speech that is cohesive, smooth, and integrated.

EXERCISE #6: USE TRANSITIONS

Choose three or four of the transition types mentioned in this chapter and apply them in your everyday conversations with others, noticing their effectiveness as you do.

TEN WORKABLE SPEECH TRANSITIONS

1. Bridge words or connective phrases

2. Prompters or triggers

3. Questions and rhetorical questions

4. Flashbacks

5. Bullet points

6. Audiovisual aids

7. Meaningful pauses

8. Physical movement

9. Humor or storytelling

10. Examples between points

CHAPTER 7

Powerhouse Endings

THE CONCLUSION IS THE most valuable part of any speech: it must be compelling and engaging, it must create anticipation, and, above all, it must be memorable.

It is in your conclusion that you will motivate your audience to commit to your call to action—to actually *respond and do something*, rather than merely spectate. And in moving your audience to commit to something, you will demonstrate your real leadership ability.

TECHNIQUES FOR CREATING A POWERHOUSE ENDING

You may want to **summarize or refer back to your key points** at the end of your speech. Tying your points together at the end

QUESTIONS FIRST, CONCLUSION LAST

Never conduct a question-and-answer period after your conclusion. It's anticlimactic. **Conduct your question-and-answer period** *before* **your conclusion.** For example, you could say, "Before I conclude my presentation, I would like to open the floor up to questions." Doing this allows you to answer questions without sacrificing the chance to use your conclusion to build momentum back up and end your speech on a strong note.

of your presentation creates a sense of cohesion and unity. It also reminds your audience of what they've just been through and can give them the sense that you have accomplished what you said you planned to accomplish at the beginning of your speech.

A great way to end a speech is to **present an emphatic challenge**—for example, "I'm urging every single one of you to take action, to get involved, and to make a difference. This will require you to make a firm decision. Let's move forward." Remember, you have the right to make this kind of appeal to your listeners, because they've essentially elected you as their leader for the duration of your presentation.

An equally good approach is to **get your audience to look toward the future.** "Success is what the future will hold for you, ladies and gentlemen, if you take part in the group involvement and teamwork we are formulating here today."

Never use the phrase "in conclusion." It's predictable and is a sure giveaway that the person speaking is an amateur.

THE BOTTOM LINE

Craft your conclusion so that it builds momentum, is compelling and memorable, and includes your call to action. In your final words to your audience, you should be instructing them to take action, take a stand, get involved, or make some other sort of commitment. Remember, every speech you give is geared toward some sort of product or outcome, and your conclusion is your last chance to get your audience on board.

EXERCISE #7: WRITE A CONCLUSION

Referring to the Six Key Factors of a Memorable Conclusion list on the following page, write a conclusion that builds your call to action.

SIX KEY FACTORS OF A
MEMORABLE CONCLUSION

To ensure that your presentation conclusions are climactic, motivating, and memorable, use these six strategies:

1. Build momentum right through the call to action.

2. Include a summary of your points.

3. Pose a sincere, direct challenge to your audience.

4. Direct your audience—with positive, acceptable control—to your call to action.

5. Conduct your question-and-answer period *before* delivering your conclusion, to maintain impact.

6. Utilize your call to action and move the audience to accept your help.

Note: In part III, we will explore further information on conclusions that build.

Eight Public Speaking Blunders to Avoid

AFTER YEARS OF COACHING speakers, I have developed a very simple and workable checklist of what to avoid when preparing, organizing, and delivering speeches and presentations of any kind to ensure that my students do not make these mistakes. If you use this checklist, you'll be well on your way to mastering public speaking. Here they are—eight public speaking blunders to avoid:

1. UNKNOWN AUDIENCE

Before preparing your presentation, get to know your audience. Gather enough information on who is attending that you know you are addressing the needs and interests of your audience in your speech. What do they like or dislike, agree with or disagree with? What do they want to know?

2. VAGUE OBJECTIVE

Make sure you have a clear understanding of *why* you are giving this particular presentation. There are key, distinct purposes to consider in preparing any speech or presentation, and you must define these before you start planning—they will dictate how you organize and deliver your words. So, before you start preparing and organizing, write down exactly what your objective is. This will ensure that your content is aligned consistently throughout your speech, from beginning to end.

3. UNKNOWN OUTCOME/PRODUCT

What is the end product you want your speech to result in? What is your call to action? Every speech must exact some type of commitment from your audience, and that commitment is yours to plan for and aim to get. Is it to make appointments to come see you? To visit your website? To purchase your book, video, or other materials after your speech? Decide what your product is before you start preparing and organizing your presentation.

4. LACK OF FLOW/SEQUENCE

Your speech must be sequenced properly so that it flows smoothly and clearly from start to finish. Your first priority in presenting is ensuring that you are understood clearly. A well-organized speech that will convey your message without distracting your audience or confusing them along the way is your goal.

THE EIGHT FATAL SPEECH BLUNDERS

1. Unknown audience

2. Vague objective

3. Unknown outcome/product

4. Lack of flow/sequence

5. Information overload

6. Insufficient support

7. Monotonous delivery

8. Disconnect from audience or message

5. INFORMATION OVERLOAD

Work with what is really important in your speech. Create concisely structured (not wordy) sentences, and do not add fillers just to occupy time. Edit, edit, edit.

6. INSUFFICIENT SUPPORT

Substantiate the points you are making with information or examples that clearly add to the validity or believability of the points you make. Your audience's demand is, *Prove it!* Without sufficient support, your important points will not receive the acceptance from your audience that you need and want.

7. MONOTONOUS DELIVERY

Vary your tone, pitch, emphasis, pace, and volume so you don't subject your audience to vocal monotony. Time your presentation and pace yourself when you practice, being aware of the speed with which you make your delivery, so that you make sure you're slowing down to emphasize points or perhaps speeding up when speaking with emotion. Refine your speech vocally until it sounds conversational and natural. (We'll go into this concept in greater depth in part II.)

8. DISCONNECT FROM AUDIENCE OR MESSAGE

There are three key connections involved in public speaking that, if violated, leave your audience disassociated from and uninvolved with your purpose or products. These are: 1) speaker connected to message; 2) speaker connected to audience; and 3) message connected to audience. If you are not connected to both your message and your audience, you won't be able to connect your message to your audience, either. More details on the three speaker connections in chapter 18.

THE BOTTOM LINE

Know these eight blunders cold, and use this chapter as a reference for your next presentation—it's guaranteed to help you avoid speech catastrophes!

KEYS TO PREPARING AND ORGANIZING ANY SPEECH

1. Fully know the audience you are presenting to.

2. Formulate the objective of your presentation.

3. Formulate the desired product or outcome of your presentation.

4. Acquire sufficient information/content about your subject.

5. Design the structure for your outline.

6. Devise an attention-getting opening.

7. Provide appropriate support sources.

8. Create a compelling and memorable conclusion.

9. Practice all visual aids.

10. If you decide to include a Q&A period, prepare for it.

11. Less is more—edit your presentation.

12. Practice! Practice some more! Attain effortlessness!

End of Part I: Practical

USING THE SEVEN EXERCISES contained in this chapter as a jumping-off point, prepare and organize a twenty-minute presentation for a group of any type and size.

Part II
Speaker
Magnetism

Magnetism: strong, attractive power or
charm; the power to influence.

CHAPTER 9

The Commanding Speaker

THROUGHOUT ALL THE YEARS I've spent coaching professionals and leaders in the artful science of public speaking, I've come to see that the most essential ingredient to creating a dynamic and impactful speech or presentation is the most powerfully simple and the most rewarding to achieve: an *authentic, true self.*

A natural, expressive, extroverted, and interested personality—regardless of the subject matter or the size of the group—is the surest way to positively attract an audience and hit the mark with a presentation.

I have never seen a false or contrived personality (what I call a "synthetic" personality) make a successful speech or presentation, because audiences are not easily fooled. With this in mind, I take all of my clients down the path of *subtractive improvement*[SM]—gains achieved through the loss of negative additives that have reduced their effectiveness as speakers. This does not mean that I am out to change you; rather, my purpose is to remove or dissolve whatever is inhibiting you or impeding your genuine personality from emerging when you make a presentation. Once you strip away these undesirables, you can achieve a comfort and effortlessness that will make you easy and fun to listen to for any audience.

Yes, there are mechanics and steps involved in preparing and organizing the outline or framework of your presentation—but to be successful throughout your career, the most essential thing is to always be yourself: unique, one of a kind, original. As long as you are authentic, as long as you are real, as long as you are fully present, you have it in you as a speaker to be compelling and impactful.

Being knowledgeable about the fundamentals covered in part I of this book is a necessity if you wish to become a No Fear Speaker; however, it is not, obviously, the entirety of the art. Speakers must use themselves as the conduit by which a message is conveyed to an audience. In this section, I will reveal how you can take control of your audience and establish yourself as a masterful, expressive, and incandescent speaker.

CREATING A COMMANDING PRESENCE: THE 5 C'S

In order to command an audience, there are five qualities you must possess—what I call the 5 C's. These five qualities distill the essence of what a commanding speaker should *be* in order to perform at their maximum potential; they're the qualities that make speakers real leaders. To be a true master of public speaking, you have to be:

1. **Comfortable.** Being comfortable means being at ease not only in any environment in which you're giving a presentation, but also with who you are. If *you* have a problem with you, then guess what? So will your audience.

2. **Caring.** Great speakers care about the welfare of the people they're talking to and talking about, and that registers with their audiences. If you felt that the person speaking to you didn't really care about you or your concerns, why would you bother to listen to them?

3. **Confident.** Think of John F. Kennedy, Winston Churchill, Ronald Reagan, and Dr. Martin Luther King, Jr. All of these people exuded a sense of absolute confidence and assurance in themselves, in their leadership missions, and in the messages they conveyed to others.

4. **Credible.** As we discussed in part I, without credibility, how can you assert yourself as a trusted figure? No one wants to waste their time listening to someone whom they find difficult to believe or devoid of honesty.

5. **Charismatic.** Charisma is the ability to influence others through one's own personal dynamism and flair. We'll go into further detail about this enviable trait later in the book, but the thing to remember about charisma is: *it can be taught.*

A MASTER AT WORK

FDR's famous radio "fireside chats" in the 1940s are an example of a truly commanding speaker at his best. Roosevelt's broadcasts brought Americans closer together when the world was in crisis, and his listeners welcomed him "into their living rooms" because his delivery made them feel as if he knew and understood them. When a speaker's delivery is executed well, members of the audience should feel as though they are being personally addressed, even if they're in a room full of people.

ACHIEVING MAGNETISM

Magnetism, as defined at the beginning of this chapter, is the ability to attract, charm, and influence the people around you. Those who have this ability are sometimes referred to as having an "attractive personality," as being "inspirational" or "influential," or as giving off a kind of "brightness"—but whatever descriptors are used, magnetism is an unmistakable magic that some individuals not only possess but positively radiate.

Charismatic people are like diamonds: they sparkle and shine, and they always stand out, even in a crowd. They seem to possess a certain special something that immediately enhances their surroundings when they enter a room. This may appear to be an innate quality, but it's not—there is a *recipe* to becoming like this, and you can learn it. Once you do, you, too will have the power to give a natural, expressive, effortless, moving, and even electrifying presentation.

Speakers who exhibit the five traits listed above—who are

LEARNING TO LOOK OUTWARD

If you have a tendency to turn inward or become withdrawn in social situations, you need to train yourself to
look outward and focus on those around you. Here's a
drill that can help:

1. Find a crowded room or large space where
   many people typically gather—a mall, down-
   town at lunchtime, a theater full of moviego-
   ers awaiting the start of a film.

2. Position yourself where you can see everyone (without being a distraction) and look
   at them—first at each individual person, one-
   by-one, and then as a collective group—until
   you can look without thinking or introverting.
   Just continue watching until you've moved
   past your reactions or thoughts and can just
   be where you are, without feeling any of the
   discomfort you started with.

3. Repeat as necessary—it should get easier
   every time!

comfortable, caring, confident, credible, and charismatic— are expressive and fully interested in the world around them. They are genuine when they unleash their ideals and principles before an audience. They are always looking ahead and outward; they're never reflective or withdrawn when around others. They take control, use supportive materials for credibility, and give their audience instructions or ask them questions. When it is appropriate, they may even relinquish control to their audiences for a time, but they are capable of taking that control back when they want to.

Commanding speakers find something to admire in those they speak to and close the distance between them and their audience by utilizing these laws of attraction. Such speakers will make an audience feel at home and create a sense of magnetic pull, through their relaxed, comfortable, and confident demeanor. They are also prepared to resolve difficulties when they arise, often without the audience's even feeling the interruption.

THE BOTTOM LINE

Magnetism can raise a person's level of communication to dynamic, memorable, and even historic proportions. The 5 C's are the qualities that great leaders employ to inspire others to take action and effect positive change—and, most important, they are qualities that can be *learned, developed, and mastered.*

EXERCISE #8: MASTER THE 5 C'S

Record (on audio or video) a two- to three-minute speech, then play it back to yourself, paying close attention to your delivery. How many of the 5 C's come across? Keep practicing!

TEN TIPS FOR BECOMING A MORE COMMANDING SPEAKER

1. Unscripted and conversational delivery naturally attracts.

2. Look, don't think! Observe everything and everyone.

3. An inspiring story from your personal experience creates impact and raises trust, and can even add a little humor to your presentation.

4. Varying your voice, body movement, pace, and attitude dissolves monotony.

5. Engaging your audience with interactions gets them involved and increases the impact of your message.

6. Expressing appropriate emotions and physicality can move your audience to take action.

7. Observe your audience and listen attentively to them during your presentation—that's the mark of a great speaker.

8. Utilizing benefit statements (statements that make the value of your intended product or outcome clear to your audience) throughout your speech enhances your reach.

(continued on next page)

(continued from previous page)

9. Always keep in mind the three key connections when practicing or delivering your speech live: 1) speaker connected to message; 2) speaker connected to audience; 3) message connected to audience.

10. Get your audience to contemplate the consequences of doing nothing about the problem, versus taking action. This concept is covered in more detail in chapter 27 "The Problem—Solution Scale."

CHAPTER 10

Becoming an Authentic Speaker

I BELIEVE THAT PEOPLE naturally feel really good being themselves, as opposed to not being themselves, and that feeling comes across when you're speaking in front of an audience. Being "authentic" means being genuine and real—tapping into the essential you. Being "synthetic," on the other hand, means being plastic, contrived, and absolutely unnatural. It's a device that some people use to get attention, but it's impossible to sustain, because it's based on something that's untrue.

Synthetic speakers put up walls between themselves and their audience. Authentic speakers knock those walls down.

You will never truly reach people using mechanisms or tricks. A person showing up fully at their presentation—*that's* what stage presence is all about.

> **Presence: the state or fact of being present, as with others or in a place.**
>
> How "there" or present are you? Are you fully "there" where you are? The more present you are, the more of yourself you give to your audience, and the more authentic your presentation becomes.

One of the most powerful realizations you can have as a public speaker is that the best thing you can do onstage is to simply be yourself and express yourself freely—be it in front of ten people or five thousand. In fact, when you're fully authentic and present, you can speak to five thousand people and it will *feel* like a one-on-one conversation with your best friend!

AUTHENTIC VS. SYNTHETIC SPEAKERS^{SM}

There are specific characteristics used for comparisons between the authentic and the synthetic speaker.

An authentic speaker is an **extroverted, expressive, interested** speaker whose presentation is **natural** and **effortless.** That speaker is **looking outward,** being who they truly are—they're "unleashed".

The synthetic speaker is *trying* to be interesting, but because they are fearful of unleashing themselves, they are very scripted, thinking about what they are going to say next, instead of about what is needed—in the moment—to drive a point home. Synthetic speakers typically try to emulate those whom they consider to be really good speakers, instead of being themselves, but because it's coming from an inauthentic place, this strategy always falls flat.

There are different degrees of "there-ness," and what I look for in my sessions with my performing artists and my speakers is the degree of "there-ness" that they exude. My goal is to help each of my clients be so "there" that they are not even tempted to think or look inward while they're presenting—to make sure that their attention is alive and fully on the audience, as though they were engaged in an engrossing conversation with them. I've found this approach to be a very effective tool in helping my clients really hit their mark.

THE BOTTOM LINE

Maintain the integrity of who you are, and don't lose sight of the ideas you embrace when you speak in public. You will never lose your audience if you never lose sight of your essential sense of truth. Be true to yourself, and your audience, in turn, will be true to you.

EXERCISE #9: STRIVE FOR AUTHENTICITY

Get into the daily practice of noticing how many of the specific authentic and synthetic speaker traits are present in your conversations with others, both on your side and on theirs. Embrace the qualities of the left column of the following chart, and be an authentic speaker.

AUTHENTIC VS. SYNTHETIC SPEAKERS

AUTHENTIC	SYNTHETIC
Extroverted	Introverted
Expressing	Impressing
Interested	Interesting
Natural	Artificial
Effortless	Forced
Reaching	Restraining
Observing	Opinionated
Looking	Thinking

CHAPTER 11

Variety vs. Monotony

IF YOU'RE LOOKING TO BORE your audience to death, I suggest that you deliver your entire speech in a monotone.

You could have written the greatest speech in the world, practiced it a zillion times, and packed the room with those who adore you—but if your voice has zero dynamics and you don't vary your inflection, chances are you'll win first prize for putting people to sleep.

When it comes to public speaking, monotony and variety are total opposites: monotony destroys a quality presentation, while variety in your voice, the tone of your speech, and your physical movements can win an audience over.

VOCAL VARIETY

People who are excited to be talking to one another automatically vary their speech, vocal patterns, pitch, tone, inflection, and volume levels. When it comes to speech, therefore, variety is a natural connector—whether you're talking to one person or to a huge group.

Vary the attitude and emotion you're expressing, and vary the rhythm and speed of your delivery, to keep your audience engaged and create better transitions to the points you wish to deliver.

SPONTANEITY AS VARIETY

Emphasizing the difference or newness of each point you make will also ensure that your audience "stays with you" and that you take them on a journey. Practiced politicians do this very well—they may repeat the same speech at every location they visit, but they manage to make it sound new on each occasion, and thus never give the audience the feeling that they've communicated the same message countless times before.

Humor—a joke or an amusing anecdote—is a great way to make sure you've injected enough variety into your presentation. Comic relief itself dissolves monotony.

PHYSICAL VARIETY

Body language, physical movement, and gestures can also be varied for dramatic purposes. The right physical movements at the right time can be used to create moments of heightened drama. Even bursting out suddenly with a thought and accompanying movement at an appropriate moment—intentionally making your audience jump out of their skin—can be effective. It's not about which particular movements you make; the point is, you can use your body as yet another tool to ensure that the involvement of your audience stays constant.

THE BOTTOM LINE

Variety, the spice of life, is the solution to keeping your presentations alive. It tells your audience that you are there with them in the moment, and that the moments you are sharing with them are spontaneous, real, and meaningful.

EXERCISE #10: PRACTICE VARIETY

You can learn to exercise variety in your speech, emotion, tempo, attitude, and body movement by experimenting with different delivery approaches at home. Here's how:

Using one simple phrase or point, practice varying the emotion and emphasis of your delivery over-and-over again. Purposely increase and decrease your volume, talking speed, and level of emotion. Try out different gestures and movements each time; then try exaggerating different words within the phrase or sentence you're practicing with. (For example, you could say, "Emphasis is key" three different ways: "*Emphasis* is key"; "Emphasis *is* key"; "Emphasis is *key*.") Record yourself, but do not practice by looking into a mirror—you want your focus to be outward, not on yourself. As you practice, you will get the sense that you're stretching your voice and body like a rubber band. This is the kind of flexibility you should strive for!

CHAPTER 12

Vocal Quality

THE QUALITY OF YOUR VOICE can either add to or detract from the impact of your presentation. When you let your speech become sloppy, it distracts your audience. A good public speaker speaks clearly and smoothly, even as they steer clear of a monotone.

BREATHING

As a singer and as someone who has coached other singers throughout my life, I understand more than most how essential **breathing** is. The framework for good vocal quality is based on regular breathing. If you're standing up onstage for any extended period of time—whether it's twenty minutes or five hours—you want to make sure that your body won't be a distraction. When you need to gasp for breath, your body is distracting you. Some of us have bodies that don't comply when we ask them for a breath while standing before an audience, so this is a skill that has to be mastered. Dancers must master it. Singers must master it. Actors must master it. And speakers must master it.

Can you master your body? Is it in good shape? When you give it an order, will it comply? These are questions to ask yourself before giving a presentation—and if your answer is no, you have work to do.

VARIETY

Variety is crucial to your ability to support and convey your message—not just because emotion and attitude keep your audience interested, but because they keep **you** from getting sloppy. There is great power in human emotion, and when you speak with passionate conviction, your voice will be at its best. Let your emotions and your attitude give fire to your speech. It will make you downright compelling.

CLARITY

Achieving **vocal clarity** does not need to mean—in fact, it *should* not mean—practicing "Speak the speech, I pray you, as I pronounced it to you trippingly on the tongue" repeatedly. Articulation is important, but so is *staying within your dialect.* If you're from Brooklyn, don't try to hide it. If you speak a Southern dialect, don't try to hide it. Don't suppress or attempt to change the way you talk. It will only make your voice (and therefore your presentation) sound forced or contrived. Words are words, no matter what accent they're delivered in—and your job is to make sure your audience hears them, not to fit your speech into some generic mold.

PERSONAL WELL-BEING

The quality of your voice and the connection it makes to your audience improves in proportion to the quality of your **physical, mental, and emotional well-being.** You really need to take care of yourself as you prepare to speak, present, or perform in any manner. As an athlete or performing artist must fine-tune their physical condition as they prepare for that special event, so, too, must a speaker make sure that they are operating at their best. What is most often ignored—but what should be primary—is your environment and the quality of people you associate with. Make it a steadfast rule never to align with negativity or people who have a bent toward destruction. Staying positive and healthy is essential to your success as a presenter.

Note: Speakers who cannot seem to present without a lot of additives like "um" or "uh" are burdened with what I call "automatic speech mechanisms" that they cannot control. Any speech habit or physical mannerism like swaying, I have found can easily be resolved in my coaching sessions to bring the speaker in control of their speech and out from under the automatic control mechanism that is controlling them and their speech.

THE BOTTOM LINE

Vocal quality reflects the quality of the speaker. Breathe easy and openly. Be healthy, and do your best to live a relatively stress-free life. Use emotion, attitude, and tonal changes, and vary your pace and tempo, throughout your speech. Do not attempt to change your dialect or cover up your accent if you have one, but do articulate so that you will be heard clearly. Practice and drill frequently, and you will speak with your own true, personal voice—one that will attract and engage your audience.

FOUR MAJOR FACTORS IN ACHIEVING VOCAL QUALITY

1. **Effective Breathing**

   - Regular, controlled breaths

2. **Vocal Variety**

   - Volume

   - Pitch/tone

   - Inflection

   - Pace, tempo, and rhythm

   - Emphasis

   - Attitude

   - Emotion

3. **Vocal Clarity**

   - Articulation

   - Dialect approach

4. **Personal Well-Being**

   - Proper nutrition

   - Vocal exercise

   - Stress-free environment

CHAPTER 13

Making Your Body Express the Message

THE BODY SHOULD FUNCTION in much the same way your vocal quality does: it should enhance and support your message, communicating without being distracting.

I believe the most natural approach for a speaker is to use their body expressively, much like a singer does during a performance. Of course, it's one thing for the singer to feel their song, but it's quite another to make the audience feel it, too. If you fail to connect with your audience, everything you do up there onstage becomes a wasted effort. If, however, you use the right combination of vocal quality and physicality, you *will* emotionally impact your audience.

AVOID CONTRIVANCE

I can't tell you how many times I've heard people assign all kinds of significance to specific physical gestures. ("Here's a defensive gesture." "Here's a nervous gesture." "Here's a confident gesture.") There may be some validity to these statements, but that doesn't mean you can just throw together a bunch of "positive" gestures and call it a day. If you think you're going to create something organic that way, you're sadly mistaken—it's not natural, and your audience will pick up on that right away.

Acting in the nineteenth century depended upon actors' assuming certain routine physical poses in order to signal to the audience the emotional state of the characters they were playing. Contrast that approach with that of the great contemporary actors—they don't assume any specific poses, but rather play their characters from a place of pure honesty. Today, that nineteenth-century style of acting would read as "campy," canned, or overblown, whereas the contemporary style reads as truthful and is therefore felt by the entire audience. Your audience doesn't want a staged performance. Don't use any artificial movements or choreography that will destroy the credibility you're working hard to earn with them.

BEST PRACTICES FOR PHYSICAL MOVEMENTS ONSTAGE

Physical movement on the whole should never be overwhelming to an audience. Simply put, it should build. I personally like to come forward toward an audience when I'm making a point and then withdraw somewhat when I'm done, in order to underscore the point and provide a natural transition to the next part of my speech.

The body has its own rhythm, and as a speaker you need to be aware of yours. If you're going to make a point, don't go off your rhythm—keep it in sync with what you're saying. Move like a singer who is in tempo with the material they are performing.

Eye contact is the most important physical trait in communication, and you should give it the highest priority during a presentation, because it has a direct bearing on how you interact with your audience. It also reveals your personality and uniqueness. To quote the famous Russian acting teacher, Constantin Stanislavski, "The eyes are the mirror of the soul." So, look at your audience. Give them the sense that you're looking at them one-on-one. Give them a sense of your soul.

THE BOTTOM LINE

Outwardly express your message with natural and appropriate physicality during your presentation. When you're authentic, you can support your message and give more personal animation to your delivery through physical movement, without being distracting to your audience.

EXERCISE #11: MASTER YOUR BODY LANGUAGE

Review the following graphic illustrations of various body language "dos" and "don'ts," then mimic them while standing in front of a mirror, so you can clearly see what it looks like when you do each one. Notice the difference between the negative postures/movements and the positive ones.

NEGATIVE BODY LANGUAGE

Clenching your hands

Wiping away sweat

Pulling at your pants

Tucking in shirt

Hands in your pockets

Playing with pointer or pen

Crossing your arms

Rubbing or scratching your nose

Pointing at your audience accusingly

Peering off aimlessly to the side

Twirling thumbs displaying boredom

Standing position back on heels

POSITIVE BODY LANGUAGE

Positive body language illustrations of a confident, comfortable, expressive, and commanding speaker.

BODY LANGUAGE: THE DOS AND DON'TS

Though I don't believe in "manufactured" poses and gestures, there are a number of gestures (and accessories) that should be avoided during a presentation, as well as some good habits that should be developed. Here's a list of dos and don'ts for your consideration.

Don'ts: Negative Physical Gestures and Presentation

- clenching your hands

- rubbing the back of your neck

- wiping away sweat

- playing with your hair

- swaying

- pulling at your pants

- tucking in your shirt

- fidgeting while sitting or standing

- picking at your skin

- clearing your throat

(continued on next page)

- putting your hands in your pockets

- clasping your hands together in front of you

- playing with a pointer or pencil

- crossing your arms

- rubbing or scratching your nose

- peering off to the side

- darting your eyes back and forth

- taking short, quick breaths

- pointing at your audience accusingly

- wearing a hat or reflective jewelry

- tightly gripping the lectern

- fiddling with jewelry or props

- wearing glasses with heavy rims or tinting that hides your face/eyes

- wearing clothes that need to be adjusted when you stand up or sit down

(continued on next page)

MAKING YOUR BODY EXPRESS THE MESSAGE

(continued from previous page)

Dos: Positive Physical Gestures and Presentation

- relaxing your arms and hands at your sides

- assuming a squared and stable body position

- tilting slightly forward

- opening your arms and hands

- making relaxed and interested eye contact with your audience

- smiling when appropriate

- peering off toward the back of the room with a determined look

- moving your body exactly, deliberately, and in a way that is appropriate to the message you wish to convey

CHAPTER 14

Humor: Entertaining Your Audience

WE ALL LOVE TO LAUGH—it's good for the soul, after all!—and using humor in your presentation can be a very effective means of winning over your audience. It breaks the ice; it disarms people and puts them in a receptive mood. Even when you're making a serious point, your audience may be more apt to get your message if it's laced with humor.

KEEP IT APPROPRIATE

You can use your audience as subject matter for humor, but you should do so only with great care, since humor can be mistaken for sarcasm. This goes back to a basic core principle: know who your audience is and what it is that they'll appreciate.

Keeping your jokes appropriate also means getting your timing right. I'm not a big proponent of telling a joke right up front when you step on stage, for example—it's a bit cliché—but it can be appropriate if it has something to do with the theme of the evening or the reason why people are there in the first place. When a joke has to do with somebody they know or something they know about, audiences generally find it funny.

KEEP IT SPONTANEOUS

You shouldn't underestimate the kinds of results that can be produced from the marriage of humor and spontaneity. That second part, however—*spontaneity*—is essential. Your jokes should occur naturally and spontaneously; that way, your audience will be surprised and delighted each time.

To all you hams out there who can't stop forcing your bad jokes on people, here's a word of caution: never try too hard to be funny, and never insert humor into a place in your speech where you think, *I'm just going to put it here so people can laugh.* It has to be a supportive element of your presentation; it has to *work* there. And it has to be organic. Remember, if you're telling a story and you're telling it well, you will be amusing and entertaining—you won't have to cram jokes into it.

KEEP IT SIMPLE

People tend to assume that making a speech humorous has to do with getting wild guffaws or letting loose a barrage of punch lines, but that's not the case. Making your speech humorous simply means making it lighthearted—it's like adding in a bit of helium to buoy your presentation and make it more accessible by keeping it from being stiff and formal.

Humor can, of course, be adapted or borrowed—but the best humor often comes out of our personal experiences. When we laugh at ourselves, we display our heart and soul, and that kind of vulnerability hits close to home for an audience every time.

THE BOTTOM LINE

I've never seen an event or a presentation that was too serious come off well. If your speech is too doom-and-gloom and too based on consequences, you will only end up turning people off. Don't force jokes down your audience's throat, of course—but do offer your

"LIGHTEN" UP

A while back, I was training a group of college teachers. Things started out a bit slow, so, in an effort to loosen things up, I told them a story from my early years as a college student: I was in philosophy class, and I was having difficulty seeing my professor's point of view on the subject of change. He told me a joke—"How many philosophy professors does it take to change a lightbulb? . . . One, but the lightbulb's got to want to change!"—which both made me laugh and allowed me to see that I was part of the problem. Now, years later, telling this story allowed my trainees to connect with me on a personal level *and* it injected some levity into the room, lightening up the session considerably. This is a great example of how humor can make us vulnerable, and resultantly, likable to our audience.

audience some entertainment value. Humor—done right—is quite often the ingredient you need to really make your presentation smoking hot.

EXERCISE #12: PRACTICE USING HUMOR

Tell an amusing story—something you've experienced personally—to one or more people. Practice the timing so it doesn't sound pushed or rushed. Do not *try* to be funny; instead, let the natural humor of the situation shine through. Note the response of your audience.

CHAPTER 15

Owning Your Presenting Space

BEFORE YOU EVEN UTTER a word of your presentation, your first step should be to fully *create* the space you will speak in. What I mean by this is that you should be *aware, perceiving, looking*—not *thinking*. Thinking is an introverted characteristic. When you go inward like that while onstage, it contracts your space— it inhibits your ability to create your own dimension and include people in your space. When you look outward, in contrast, you can deliver your concepts with energy and emotion to your audience because you have created the space in which to do it.

EXPAND YOUR REACH

Space is defined by dimension, and you have to view it from where you are, and in the dimensions you are creating. You are there in that space, owning that space. That's very important. You might think "space" is a relative term—something undefined—but it is vital to your presentation. If you look out and all the way back to the last row of the audience while you're onstage, you are opening up the entire room.

The area to which you direct your attention can reach as far out as you want it to. In fact, the performers I work with learn to take command of the stage and really deliver their message by opening up their space so it's nice and big. Your space can even extend beyond the confines of the physical dimensions of the room where you're presenting, if you want it to. Try it—it can make a huge difference!

OBSERVE YOUR SURROUNDINGS

I also advise my clients to really get a good sense of the room in which they're presenting. The first thing you should do when you enter the room is to take a good look around. Observe color and texture and lines and form. Notice what people are wearing and what they look like. Connect with your space.

THE BOTTOM LINE

For a speaker, space is key. Before you start talking, you need to make sure you are aware of every aspect of the space you are presenting in, and you need to make sure your presentation reaches all of those areas. Perception is key—if you can't perceive the space you are in, you are not going to be able to communicate with your audience.

LEARNING TO OWN YOUR SPACE

If you need help perceiving, creating, and owning your space during your presentations, try this:

1. Arrive at your presentation location early—before anyone else arrives—and walk around the room and stage.

2. Look over every object in the room, taking note of the colors, shapes, sizes, textures, and anything else that interests you about each thing you look at.

3. Notice how your awareness of the space you're in increases and your feelings of nervousness decrease as you familiarize yourself with your surroundings.

I have seen speakers fully calm down prior to their introductions—and occupy their space more powerfully once they get on stage—when they've made use of this drill. Give it a try!

EXERCISE #13: PRACTICE OWNING YOUR SPACE

Visit the space where you are going to present next (if that's not possible, go to any presentation room in your vicinity) and look at every object in the room. Really observe and notice exactly everything you see. The key to this is really looking and not forming an opinion of what it might be, but what it is exactly in detail. This drill focuses you on looking, not thinking. For example "I see an old speaker system in the room" is not correct. "I see two corded grey microphones peering out from the top of a wooden inclined podium tabletop..." says that you are perceiving the room in detail.

Describe in detail everything you are seeing (with no opinions), until you feel you are present and fully there in that space.

CHAPTER 16

Preparing Mentally and Physically Before Your Presentation

WANTING TO INSPIRE PEOPLE and actually being able to do so are two different things. But, there *are* preparatory steps you can take that will help you hit your target—they will help ensure you deliver your speech with the wind at your back, and that you're in absolute command and control of your environment and the material you're delivering.

I'm not talking about acquiring material for your speech, creating an outline, or answering any of the questions I had you ask yourself in part I regarding the design of your presentation. I'm talking about how you get yourself into "the zone"—a state of mind that will allow you to achieve excellence during your presentation.

SPEAKING AS A PERFORMANCE ART

Let me start by stating a very simple and powerful, yet totally underappreciated, truth: *speaking is a performance art, and therefore you must have command over the material that you are using if you wish to master it.*

Other artists besides Michelangelo may have wanted to sculpt a marble *David* for the city of Florence, but only Michelangelo's work was chosen. Why? Because he knew how to sculpt marble well. If he'd had inferior skills—if his execution hadn't matched his vision—then who in the world would have regarded him or his work with any favor?

Musicians practice their music, dancers practice their moves, and athletes practice their plays again and again and again, until they become second nature. Look at professional football players: they know their *X*'s and *O*'s, and they run plays until they're so ingrained in the players' minds and bodies that when game time comes, their full attention is totally focused on their opponents and on the game itself, not on themselves.

TAKE COMMAND

So, in order to be an inspiring speaker, you must first really **know your material.** Just like an actor, you have to have your lines down—know every line and move so well that no part of your speech will be a stop or an impediment to your presentation. Your speech must *flow*.

Once you've practiced your speech—maybe recorded it, maybe reviewed the videos to see what you could do better and then tried again—you have to move on to your space. Now that you have command of your material, you have to gain command of your environment.

In order to do this, you must get into communication with the room by employing the tools we discussed in chapter 15. Look at everything. This is *your* space. Now **make your point of view expansive**—extend your perception of distance and look way beyond the last row of your audience, all the way to outside the building. You want to have a sense of the bigness of the space you're in. To achieve this goal, you might want to get there before people arrive, particularly if it's a very large space and you're on a platform stage. That's the way to really connect with the room where you're going to be.

Let's say people have filed into the room and taken their seats. The MC is going to introduce you, and you're at the point where you're ready to go on. Rather than getting nervous, assume the position of being an *eager* speaker—a performer who is anticipating that the audience can't wait for them to get out there. You must *own* that room; you must think of the people out there as *your* people. *You* are their leader, and that's why they are there. Now you have to make sure that you are giving them every reason in the world to follow you with confidence.

LOOSEN UP

From a physical standpoint, you want to be mobile and flexible while you present. This is why some actors choose to do mild stretching exercises in the green room or in the dressing room before they walk on stage. **Limbering up your body** before your presentation can physically and mentally energize you, as well as

BEFORE YOUR PRESENTATION MAKE SURE YOU . . .

- Get sufficient sleep

- Eat healthy foods

- Hydrate

- Stretch to limber up

- Take deep, invigorating breaths

- Know what and where all your presentation tools are, and make sure they are all operational

- Assess the room by perceiving everything in it

- Notice things you like about the individuals in your audience and the room itself

- Smile genuinely

- Admire your audience (and continue to do so throughout and after your presentation!)

help you make certain that your body will be working in concert with your aims and purposes once you get up before your audience.

THE BOTTOM LINE

It doesn't matter whether I'm speaking, acting, or singing—when I know my character, when I know my audience, when I've familiarized myself with my space, when I've limbered up, when I know my material inside and out, backward and forward, *then* I am ready to connect. At that point, I'm no longer thinking about anything else but engaging in my performance. Once I'm standing there before my audience, all consideration and self-talk is extinguished. It's only me, my audience, and the task at hand.

Public speaking is a performance art, and, as with any other performance art, there are a number of things you can do to get yourself in the zone for it. Once you are in front of your audience, however, the practice is *over*. If you have fully rehearsed and prepared—if your mind is ready and your body is limber—then you will be ready to do the one thing you're there to do: unleash yourself before the people who came to hear you, and ignite them with your message!

EXERCISE #14: MAKE A MENTAL AND PHYSICAL PREPARATION CHECKLIST

Make a checklist of all the mental and physical factors you need to keep in mind before a presentation, and go over it item-by-item before your next speaking engagement.

End of Part II: Practical

APPLYING WHAT YOU'VE LEARNED about authentic speaking, vocal quality, and body language do's and don'ts in this section, create a two- to three-minute presentation about how you plan to achieve your goals in the next year.

Optional: record it and play it back as many times as you feel is necessary to help you arrive at a comfortable, natural delivery. Note the before and after.

Part III
Moving Your Audience

Inspire: to animate, influence, impel, or arouse a feeling or thought in others.

CHAPTER 17

The Art of Inspiring Others

HOW DO YOU GET TO THE place where you can inspire people by giving a speech? You start out by *really* believing in what you're saying—by having *conviction* about what you're expressing and being whole and undiluted about the principles you're teaching your audience. You're getting them to *see something* they haven't seen before. You're moving your audience by getting them to discover and explore while you deliver. It's an education.

INSPIRATION STARTS WITH YOU

Certainly, *you* have to be inspired in order to inspire others. Leadership is about inspiration; it's about leading your audience to do something and making them feel like it's worth it. If you're not excited about your topic, you can't expect them to be.

> ## MAPPING THE FUTURE
>
> Inspirational speakers get their audiences to change their minds not only by predicting consequences but also by offering alternative visions of the future. Think Susan B. Anthony in her rousing 1873 speech, "On Women's Right to Vote," which brilliantly lays out the reasons why women, as US citizens, *should* have the right to vote. Think John F. Kennedy in his message to Congress in 1961, when he challenged the American people to put a man on the moon by the end of the decade. Think Ronald Reagan in 1987 at the Brandenburg Gate when he challenged Mikhail Gorbachev to tear down the Berlin Wall. Think Dr. Martin Luther King, Jr., in 1963 on the steps of the Lincoln Memorial, delivering his "I Have a Dream" speech. These are powerful examples of people who shared their visions for how the future could be—and made a real difference in the world.

MOTIVATING THE UNMOTIVATED

When I'm sitting in an audience, I *want* to be taken somewhere—I'm *willing* to follow the speaker wherever they take me, as long as they keep me interested. And most people are like me. A good 80 percent of people in any audience—a majority—really want to change. But then there are the 20 percent or so who not only aren't interested in changing but are actively doing their darnedest not to.

So, what I like to do is to get people to understand the consequences of their *inaction*. If you can make them understand what will happen if they continue to do nothing—if you can really make them see what a difference it will make if they act—you can lead them toward movement and transformation. You want that lightbulb to turn on in people's minds.

THE BOTTOM LINE

If you want to inspire people, you have to *take them somewhere*, *wake them up*, and *show or express something to them* that will galvanize them to act.

CHAPTER 18

The Three Essential Connections

THERE ARE THREE CONNECTIONS every performing artist—including public speakers—must make when they step onto a stage if they want to effectively communicate their message.

CONNECTING WITH YOUR MESSAGE

The thing you must do as a presenter is *connect with your own message*. You must have a passion for your material; you must believe in the words you're speaking.

Why is this so imperative? Because credibility starts with you. If you have no understanding of or passion behind what you're saying, there is no chance that your audience will, either. You have to have a real connection with your presentation and the message you're trying to convey if you wish to make a real impact.

CONNECTING WITH YOUR AUDIENCE

The second thing you must do as a presenter is *connect with your audience*. You must establish a rapport with and feel a real respect and affinity for your audience, and your audience must feel a real respect and affinity for you.

Being a performer is a kind of alchemical process whereby your thoughts and emotions are transmuted and instantaneously picked up by the watching audience. But it's not a one-way street: you must also resonate with that audience—they must feel that you care about them, and that you're in tune with whom they are.

When you begin a presentation, there is a gulf between you and your audience, and your job is to bridge that gulf. If you don't engage and reach out to your audience in a welcoming manner, you'll never be able to cross that distance and communicate your message. This is where knowing your audience (covered in part I) comes in handy. The better your knowledge of whom you're addressing, the better your chances of making a connection with them.

CONNECTING YOUR MESSAGE TO YOUR AUDIENCE

The third thing you must do as a presenter is *connect your message to your audience*.

You cannot make this connection until the other two connections are already established. Once you've mastered your message and successfully reached out to your audience, however, this last connection should form naturally—your audience should be receptive to your message. All you have to do now is deliver it to them.

THE ESSENTIAL CONNECTIONS

1. Speaker to message

2. Speaker to audience

3. Message to audience

THE BOTTOM LINE

Delivering an effective presentation requires connecting with your message, connecting with your audience, and connecting the two (audience and message) to each other. Without all three connections, your presentation can't succeed—but if you meet all three conditions, you will achieve authenticity and a real, naturally arrived-at communication through conversation, and your message will hit its mark!

EXERCISE #15: PRACTICE THE THREE CONNECTIONS

Practice these three connections in your everyday conversations—at home and at work—until you truly feel the benefit and importance of the first two to the last.

Follow-up drill: Consciously make these three connections in your next presentation.

CHAPTER 19

Captivating Your Audience with Storytelling

WHAT'S THE DIFFERENCE between "There are many children in the Congo going hungry" and "I'll never forget being in war-torn Congo—witnessing firsthand the deprivation of hundreds of children, and feeding them life-nourishing food that I obtained at my own great peril"?

The difference is *story*. And the difference it makes is between something dry and airless and something compelling, electric, and laden with deep emotion.

DRAWING IN YOUR AUDIENCE

The moment you begin to tell a story, you involve your audience—you take them on an artfully painted and controlled journey. A well-crafted story allows your audience to connect to you emotionally, as well as through the sensory experiences of sight, taste, feeling, and smell.

Storytelling is also an opportunity to build suspense. You can even play with the audience by letting them guess what happens next in your tale. Think back to the 1930s and '40s, when an entire generation of Americans sat by the radio for hours, mesmerized by the intrigue and enchantment of stories such as *The Shadow* and *Dick Tracy*. The actors on those shows were not merely voices in a box—they were powerful storytellers who held their fans' attention captive solely through their ability to stoke those people's imaginations.

MASTERING STORYTELLING ESSENTIALS

To be a great storyteller, you must understand the essential factors of the process. Once you've mastered these keys, you may be rewarded with the enviable ability to hold an audience breathless and on the edge of their seats. These essentials consist of the following:

- Describing your experience in a detailed way that entices the audience to be a part of your journey.

- Displaying appropriate and honest emotion that underlines and illustrates your narrative.

- Using varied vocal qualities and facial expressions (without being distracting) to augment your points.

- Honing your timing to punctuate key moments or points.

- Weaving natural (not forced) humor into your story.

Whether your story is humorous or deadly serious, it must be intimate, personal, and above all honest if it is to fulfill the objective of increasing your credibility. Remember that the element of entertainment can serve a speaker very well and should therefore not be taken lightly or dismissed as superfluous. Even profound subjects may produce a listless response from an audience when they are taken up by a mediocre speaker, whereas a masterful speaker can rouse their listeners to respond to almost any topic at all.

THE BOTTOM LINE

Telling a story can breathe life into your presentation. If you practice your storytelling—perfecting your timing, letting it flow naturally, and implementing the key elements listed above—it can become your most effective means of supporting your points and your agenda.

EXERCISE #16: TELL A STORY

Find someone to tell a story to, and use all the ingredients discussed in this chapter to describe everything so thoroughly that your listener sees, hears, feels, smells, and tastes every aspect of it. Note how your listener or audience responds to it.

WHY STORYTELLING?

- Captivates your audience with creative descriptions

- Supports your points with credibility

- Attracts the audience to you and your message

- Motivates your audience with emotion and purpose

- Narratives convert the dull and dry into excited sensations

- Audiences remember them

- Develops and enhances the three speaking connections (speaker to message; speaker to audience; message to audience)

THE INGREDIENTS OF GREAT STORYTELLING

- The three vital audience connections of any performance (speaker to message; speaker to audience; message to audience)

- A lively, descriptive narrative

- Outward expression of appropriate emotion

- Outward expression of appropriate physical movement

- Mastering of vocal quality

- Timing and variety

- The lesson learned/moral of the story

CHAPTER 20

Interaction: The Key to Audience Involvement

IN MY EXPERIENCE, EVERY audience likes to play. What do I mean by that? Simple: when an audience is invited to participate in a presentation, they tend to be happier and more satisfied than they are when they are expected to remain mere spectators. Through interaction, they're able to "return the ball," so to speak—able to demonstrate their understanding of the information they've received and perhaps even exhibit how it can be put into practice in the real world.

Allowing your audience in on the game gets them out of their seats and onto the playing field, which in the end means you're making a far greater impact. Participation makes your message more real and therefore applicable—and makes the audience, who now have a better idea of how a concept works, feel more confident about what they've learned.

I personally love to get out among my audience while they're doing an exercise, "twin them up" into pairs, and then turn it around so that Twin One becomes Twin Two, and vice versa. This can be done with a small group or a large one—even with a really large group. If I'm presenting to a particularly big group, I like to have other supervisors or people who are ready to assist on hand, just in case I need them, but this tactic really can work with an audience of any size.

QUALITY CONTROL

Every speaker's responsibility is to make sure an audience understands the information they're receiving *and* can effectively apply the tools they've just learned to a real-world situation. I know of no better way to meet this responsibility than by testing it out yourself with your own audience, in your very own "laboratory" setting. By having the audience role-play, you can become the supervisor or "quality controller," observing the exercises you're having them engage in and gauging their efficacy.

INTERACTION OPTIONAL

If I want to show my audience a coaching tip that requires volunteers, I may bring audience members up, but it has to be optional—I always *ask* for volunteers, never demand them. You want to let your audience know that they're not obligated to participate. Luckily, there are always at least a couple of people in any audience who are willing to come up onstage.

Audience interaction is less likely to work in a keynote speech or a promotional presentation, but it's generally appropriate in pretty much any other type of presentation—particularly one that needs to demonstrate or illustrate to the audience a practical application of the speaker's subject, beyond rote theory.

THE BOTTOM LINE

Interaction can be a major component of your presentation: it not only gives the audience a tangible sense of what you're talking about but also throws them into *doing* it. When you allow audiences to participate in your presentation, you heighten your credibility, give your audience confidence, and raise the whole value of your training.

EXERCISE #17: INVOLVE YOUR AUDIENCE

Come up with a drill or skill-building exercise that supports the main message of your presentation and actively involves your audience.

CHAPTER 21

Handling a Difficult Audience

"HOW DO YOU HANDLE A difficult or rowdy audience?" I get this question a lot. The usual response from a speaker to such an audience is resistance—but over the years, I've learned that such resistance *only creates persistence*. Instead of dealing with a heckler by hurling insults back, a speaker should adopt the strategy used in martial arts: rather than trying to block the opposing force head-on, they should redirect its course and move the focus in the direction they want it to go in, which is back to the subject at hand.

RESISTANCE IS FUTILE

I was trained by a mentor who, early in his career, had vegetables thrown at him by audiences in Hyde Park, London—and from him I learned early on that when it comes to performing before

LEARNING TO GO WITH THE FLOW

If you can teach yourself to move with an attack, reaction, or distraction from an audience, rather than resisting it, you'll always be able to continue your presentation without calling attention to any interruptions that might otherwise stall or derail your speech.

An excellent example of a good way to handle a disruption is that of a salesman presented with an objection like "I don't have the money for something like this." An inexperienced salesperson might try to argue with the client and convince them that they're wrong—but an effective salesperson would acknowledge their statement and move on: "I understand it can be costly, Mr. Jones, but allow me to show you how this will benefit your family . . . "

The lesson here is not to get into resisting disruptions, but rather to experience and then redirect them so that you retain control of the conversation. It takes some time to master, but with practice it will eventually come to you naturally.

an audience, it doesn't help to resist anything. When you resist something, you make it more than what it is. Essentially, when you push against something, it pushes back at you even harder.

So, just as a nonstick surface refuses to let substances stick to its surface, the confident speaker refuses to let disruptions stick to their presentation and break their momentum. The person or persons trying to get your attention should be acknowledged and not scolded—you don't want to ignore your audience or make them wrong, and you don't want to waste precious time arguing—but that doesn't mean you have to agree with them, either. You can hold your ground without becoming defensive.

DO YOUR HOMEWORK

There is another factor to consider in this rowdy-crowd equation, however, and that factor is *you*. Consider this example: Think back to a time when you were in grade school and you were hoping that your teacher wouldn't call on you. You were probably saying under your breath, "Please don't call on me. Please don't call on me." Why? Well, probably because you weren't prepared and you hadn't done your homework, right? But the more desperate you were to escape your teacher's notice—the more you *resisted*—the more likely you were to be the first one to get called on.

So the lesson here is, if you're prepared and you know your material, you're less likely to encounter resistance from an audience. You have to be prepared for all contingencies. You have to ask yourself, "What happens if . . . ?" Simply asking and answering that question will make you far more prepared to deal with anything that might arise than you otherwise would be.

MAKE YOUR AUDIENCE FEEL HEARD

Here's another observation for you to chew on: people want to know that you've heard them. When an audience becomes difficult, it's often because they feel that you're creating divisiveness in some way—that you haven't really assessed your audience, that you don't understand what their needs are, what their wants are, and what they're interested in.

If you know your audience and you know what your presentation's purpose is (remember APP—audience, purpose, product), even a rabble-rousing, riotous kind of group shouldn't present a problem for you—you should be able to walk into any group setting and give your presentation without a hitch. If you know you're going to get strong vocal feedback, *allow* for that. Don't try to stop it. Let the audience know up front that you're open to comments: "I want you all to know that I am here to address every one of your needs and concerns, and I'm absolutely open to hearing everything that you have to say." If you do this, I guarantee your audience will listen to you.

THE BOTTOM LINE

Audiences are difficult only when you haven't done your job. There aren't any bad audiences; there are only bad speeches or bad speakers that haven't fully connected to their audience. When you're speaking before a group, the power to win over the people you're addressing lies with *you*. Approach your audience with this philosophy, and you'll have them in your back pocket.

EXERCISE #18: PRACTICE STAYING ON TASK

Practice having conversations in environments that are noisy and distractive. Use the "no resistance, no persistence" approach, and don't cut your conversation short—get your message across. Note what happens after several practice runs.

CHAPTER 22

Mastering the Art of Answering Questions During a Presentation

AS STATED IN PART I, you should *never* end a presentation with a Q&A session. You don't want to deliver a truly wonderful, powerful presentation only to have it become anticlimactic at the end simply because your Q&A period slowed your drive and momentum. If you're going to open up the floor for questions during your presentation, you want to do so *prior* to the conclusion of your speech—that way you can end things on a strong note, with your call to action.

MAINTAIN YOUR MOMENTUM

You want the Q&A portion of your presentation to build, not fizzle, which is why you should *always answer questions in the direction of a call to action*. Don't get too cerebral or too detailed in your responses; don't get into a back-and-forth debate with anyone in the audience.

ANSWERING QUESTIONS IN THE DIRECTION OF A CALL TO ACTION

Let's say you were delivering a promotional presentation of a company's product or service to a group of potential buyers at a networking or business meeting, and someone in the audience asked you, "How much do you charge for your services?" It would not be practical to answer the question, since you would likely have no relevant, personalized information about the asker—which means you would be hard-pressed to make a sound guess at what a fair price might be for them. So, instead of making up a number, what you should do is say, "Thank you for asking that question. Something like that would actually be best determined after a one-on-one interview, so we could come up with the most effective plan and the most cost-effective solution for your specific company. If I stated a price with no knowledge of your specific needs, I might end up overcharging you, and that certainly is not beneficial to you or ethical for me. If you're interested in getting a real price quote, let's schedule a time to get together and come up with something that will address your exact needs."

There's always a way to steer the conversation back toward your product or call to action. If there's someone in the audience who's asking a lot of questions that require long answers or are pulling you off-message, don't let yourself get distracted or frustrated—instead, use their curiosity as an opportunity to make a connection, especially if the product you're going for is designed to get your audience to make appointments with you.

PREPARE YOUR AUDIENCE

You should always give your audience *specific directions or instructions on how you would like to take their questions* at the beginning of your presentation, so they know up front whether or not it's okay to interrupt your speech. If there will be a Q&A period at a designated time, tell them that. If you think many of their questions will be answered during the presentation, let them know that as well. Whatever the case may be, it's important to give your audience specific instructions from the very beginning.

OTHER BEST PRACTICES FOR
RECEIVING QUESTIONS

You have to be able to *listen* to a question and make sure that you're *clarifying* what it means before you answer it—and if you think there's a possibility that not everyone in the audience has heard what the question is, be sure to repeat it so that everyone understands the answer you give. You want to be inclusive; don't leave everyone out except the person who posed the question.

Do your best to take questions in the order of hands raised, so you let your audience know you're not playing favorites—and

> **Audience blind spot: an area of your audience that you purposely ignore because you feel that someone sitting there may be confrontational, a competitor, or distracting for you.**
>
> If you ignore an area of the room or even a single person in your audience, the rest of your audience will surely pick up on it. As we discussed in the previous chapter, resistance only creates persistence. Be fully open to your entire audience for questions, and you'll be able to handle any questions that come your way.

before taking a second question from someone, make sure you hear from those people who haven't yet had a chance to ask something. (In other words, don't let one person ask all the questions if other people have their hands up.) Don't develop what I call "audience blind spots," where it appears as though you're trying not to look at someone or overlooking an entire section of the room—you should look at everyone in the room, be open, and be actively inclusive.

Never claim to know something you don't know—and if there are people in your audience who can help you answer something, let them! For example, if I don't know the answer to a question and I have a specialist in the audience—say it's a legal question and I have an attorney there—then I'll use the power of delegation and defer to them. This takes the pressure off you, and it can also build your credibility with your audience.

HANDLING THE PRESS

When dealing with the press, you're encountering a *different* kind of Q&A, because (in most cases) they are there not to learn from you but to scrutinize you—their entire intent is to get as much sensationalism out of you as possible. With this in mind, you must, must, must, be prepared with your statements if you know there will be press at your presentation, so you answer only those questions that embrace the issues that you want the public to know about. It takes training and coaching to learn how to answer the press's questions well, but once you've mastered it, you will flourish under the glare of the spotlight.

THE BOTTOM LINE

Q&A sessions must enhance (not distract from) the product of your presentation. If you employ the tactics described here, you will be able to use Q&A's to connect with your audience and build toward a compelling call to action at the end of your presentation.

EXERCISE #19: PRACTICE FIELDING QUESTIONS

Put together a small group at your home or office, give them a short speech, and then have them ask you questions. Using the Eight Tips for Answering Questions Like a Pro list on the following page, as well as the other advice offered in this chapter, practice answering each question smoothly and confidently.

EIGHT TIPS FOR ANSWERING QUESTIONS LIKE A PRO

- Instruct the audience at the outset regarding your Q&A agenda.

- Maintain eye contact with your audience and include everyone.

- Take questions in the order in which hands are raised.

- In larger crowds, repeat the question asked.

- Clarify each question to make sure you understand what's being asked.

- If you don't know the answer to a question, say so.

- Increase your credibility by delegating questions to appropriate panel speakers or audience attendees.

- Never end your speech with a Q&A period; ask for audience questions before delivering your carefully crafted conclusion.

CHAPTER 23

Smart Uses of Visual Aids

THE KEY WORD FOR YOU to understand in the term "visual aid" is "aid," which means simply "assistance". A visual aid is just that—something that can assist you in your presentation. It is *not* something to be used to direct your speech. Unfortunately, however, many speakers don't understand this distinction, and they make the mistake of letting their visual aids run the show.

KEEP YOUR HANDS ON THE WHEEL

Let me be clear about this: visuals, audios, handouts, illustrations, or whatever you might use to enhance or support your communication and message should *never* substitute, replace, or upstage you. *You're* the one using those visuals, and you should use them according to the time and rhythm of *your* presentation. Never surrender control of the flow and direction of your speech to your PowerPoint slides.

Visuals can help you get your audience to feel something—for example, a picture of an earthquake victim in Haiti, if you're fundraising, *can* generate empathy—but they can't evoke the level of emotion that you can by speaking directly to your audience in your own voice. In the end, whatever emotion your presentation evokes must come from you, and the visual is there only to echo or emphasize your message. Visuals should function in much the same way music would: they should be secondary elements of your presentation, there to amplify or underscore the message you're delivering, but not to become a source of distraction.

Keep in mind that a visual aid is most effective when it is, in fact, *visual*. The less copy you have on a visual slide, the better off you'll be. The visual itself should express and illustrate the point *you're* making—it shouldn't make the point itself. Your audience should be looking at your visual while they're *listening to you*. If you put up a bunch of copy, they'll be too busy reading to listen to you.

Remember, anything that distracts your audience from your message is an enemy of your presentation. Everything you say, do, or show while you're up on that stage should support the message you're delivering. You want your visuals to be dynamic and action-oriented, rather than what someone might call "projected wallpaper." At the same time, never underestimate the power of understatement. A single, compelling picture can sometimes do more to move an audience that fifty photos would. You don't want to inundate them with too much.

EFFECTIVE VISUAL AIDS

A number of types of visual aids can be used to enhance your presentation, such as:

- Statistics, pie charts, and graphs

- Before-and-after images

- Photos of people or groups expressing emotions relevant to your presentation

- Noteworthy quotes

- A short list with a suitable image to accompany it

- A visual rendering of a proposed project

- Short (high-quality) video footage with excellent sound clarity

- A brief overview of the presentation, featuring your company logo

- A call-to-action page that ends the presentation and directs your audience to their next step (also featuring your company logo)

- Anything else you can think of that will increase the impact of your presentation— be creative!

LOGISTICAL CONSIDERATIONS

To ensure that you don't lose control of your presentation to your visual aids, try coming up with a visual aid checklist. Make sure you have a backup plan in case of a technological error or failure. Maybe this means bringing along an extension cord or additional batteries; maybe it means bringing your own microphone (I always have two or three at my disposal in case one goes out). This may sound extreme, but the fact of the matter is, no one can ever know exactly what's going to happen in the course of a presentation. What if the sound cuts off? What if the lights go out? What if your computer drops your Internet connection? What then? In the words of the Boy Scouts, "Be prepared."

It's also best to check whether everyone can clearly see your visual aids from everywhere in the room you'll be presenting in—if you don't check, you may end up hearing complaints in the middle of your presentation. The solution to this issue is simple: just sit in different corners of the room prior to your speech, and look at different aspects of the space you're presenting in, to make sure everyone's going to have a clear view. Then, once you're onstage, be aware of where you're standing—I've seen speakers block their own visuals by walking between their screen and their projector, causing a huge shadow to appear across the screen while they're speaking, and it's incredibly distracting.

Have your clicker in hand, but don't let it be a distraction for you or your audience. And if you're using a laser pointer on your screen, please, use it correctly. You don't want it moving all over the place—you want it directing your audience's attention.

Above all, you want to practice these techniques so that you're fully prepared. But when you do practice, do it in such a way that you get the audience's viewpoint on your visuals.

VISUAL AID CHECKLIST

Before your presentation, create a visual aid checklist like this one to ensure that you have everything you need and have done everything you can to ensure that things will go smoothly:

- ❏ Visuals are appropriate to the venue and clearly add to, not distract from, my presentation.

- ❏ Visuals are simple and easy to read and understand.

- ❏ Visuals are displayed where all can see without straining.

- ❏ Visuals are in correct sequence.

- ❏ If I experience technical difficulties, I have a backup plan for my visuals.

- ❏ I have a checklist of all necessary materials (handouts, markers, projector equipment, etc.), and I have gone through it and checked everything off.

- ❏ I have a cross-index in my speech outline showing me 1) when to direct the audience to a visual and 2) when to move on to my next visual.

(continued on next page)

(continued on from previous page)

❏ I have done one or more practice runs of my presentation with my visual aids to ensure confident use, timing, sequence, and logistics.

❏ I am using my visuals; they are not using me. I dictate the flow and movement of my speech, and I have the freedom to make adjustments throughout my presentation, if necessary.

THE BOTTOM LINE

Visual aids can enhance your presentation—but you should never allow them to dictate the pace, rhythm, or sequence of your presentation, or to become a distraction. Use your visuals not as the heart of your presentation, but as a support. *You* are the heart of your presentation.

EXERCISE #20: CREATE A VISUAL AID

Create a PowerPoint slideshow that follows the rule of using primarily visuals and only minimal copy.

CHAPTER 24

Maintaining the Look of Success

THE SET, THE PODIUM, the *platform*, any *handouts* you're using with your presentation, and your *look* are all part of an image that you're conveying and therefore constitute a form of nonverbal communication between you and your audience. As such, these details need to be attended to. If you neglect them, you run the risk of allowing them to become distractions that will interfere with your message.

CONTROLLING YOUR IMAGE

In order to present the right image to your audience, you have to have control of your environment—and that includes you. Keep in mind that dressing upscale gives your presentation a higher degree of legitimacy. When choosing an outfit, factor in color coordination and the style of your dress. Avoid wearing hats, tinted glasses, and reflective jewelry when you're going to be onstage—and if you have long hair, fix it so it will stay out of your face.

Visual aids, as we discussed in the last chapter, need to be displayed properly, without interference. Make sure that the room you're presenting in has sufficient lighting and is arranged in a way that will allow everyone in it to see the stage clearly. Which brings me to my next point: it's *your* responsibility to make sure everything runs smoothly, so come up with your own checklist for your needs and for proper stage management (everything having to do with the set, the room, and you).

Remember, your setup should be logical and follow a natural flow—and it's your job to make sure that everything is where it should be before you go up on that stage and begin speaking.

THE BOTTOM LINE

Every element of your presentation requires your own personal attention, from your hair and clothing to the room temperature and refreshment table. Check every detail beforehand, and you can begin speaking knowing that your look, your room, and all the materials in it are well integrated and properly in place for your dynamic presentation to come off like a million bucks!

NINE STEPS TO PROJECTING A PROFESSIONAL IMAGE AT A PRESENTATION

1. Make sure that your visual aids are displayed properly and are neither cumbersome nor overly flashy.

2. Perform a sound test prior to speaking to ensure that you'll be clearly heard at the correct volume level and with the right tonality—static, feedback, muffled sound, etc., needs to be addressed *before* your presentation begins.

3. Whether you're in a large venue or a small one, it's crucial that the room have sufficient lighting and be arranged so people will be able to see you and your visual aids without a distracting glare or insufficient lighting.

4. Check the room temperature: Is it too hot or too cold? It's important that the audience be comfortable while you're talking.

5. Set up your merchandise table properly at the back of the room so that it's accessible without being an obstruction or disrupting the people entering or exiting.

(continued on next page)

(continued from previous page)

6. Create a checklist for everything relevant to your presentation—including your clothing and props, your set, the room, name tags, the registration table, the refreshment table, the video camera(s) being used to record your speech, the sound equipment, etc.—and go through it before your presentation.

7. Figure out your presentation logistics prior to the event date so you understand where things will be set up and can make sure that they flow well from one speech section to the other.

8. Make sure that your look, your room, and all the materials in it are well integrated and properly in place—your presentation should adhere to the same high-class standards a multimillion-dollar concert production would.

9. The most important component of your presentation is *you*—your look, your expressions, your confident walk and pose, and your smile—so make sure you put your best foot forward!

CHAPTER 25

The Power of the Camera in Increasing Impact

I'VE OBSERVED A CERTAIN phenomenon that happens with a number of people: they look at a camera, and suddenly they turn into Bambi—frozen, like they're caught in the blinding headlights of an oncoming Mack truck. Any confidence they seemed to possess quickly melts away, and they are left devastated, intimidated, and completely paralyzed.

CHANGE YOUR PERSPECTIVE

The secret to transforming your on-camera presence from a liability into an asset lies in *recognizing the distance between you and the camera*.

Distance is a very important element in communication. When you sit down to talk to someone, you automatically recognize that there is a certain amount of space between you. Maybe it's a few feet, maybe a few yards—the point is, you have some separation from that person. Without sufficient distance, you may feel boxed in, too close to the person you're speaking with—like your personal space is being invaded.

People who go stiff when the red light goes on do so because they experience only the camera's intrusion. That's what leaves them with a look of sheer terror on their face. When you can recognize the distance between you and the lens, however, you can recognize that there's a different point of view in front of you—and that simple shift in perspective can change everything.

TREAT THE CAMERA LIKE A PERSON

You should consider the camera much as you would an audience. I tell my students to talk to the camera as though it's a person—to look at it and ask it a few questions ("Would you like a glass of iced tea? How about a cup of coffee? Are you comfortable?"). Before you even turn the camera on, have a *conversation* with it. Pose questions to the lens the way you would to another human being. Soon enough you'll get a sense of looking at that camera as if you're waiting for an answer—a technique that will allow you to be totally real and natural and to create a very real connection between yourself and others at the other end of the camera's eye, no matter if it's one person or millions.

KEEP IT SIMPLE

Personally, I like to let go of the fact that there's even a camera on me when I'm giving a presentation. Yes, it's good to know if you're

TIPS FOR BEING ON CAMERA

- Recognize the distance between you and the camera to create openness.

- Let your eyes tell the story and express what you feel—the most expressive body language is eye contact, and the camera loves it.

- Speak to the camera in a natural, conversational tone, as if you are talking to a friend.

- Practice, record, and play back your on-camera speech, paying attention to whether it gives the feeling of a natural, person-to-person conversation.

- Don't forget about the technical aspects—make sure you have perfect lighting, high-quality definition, and great sound clarity and depth before you record the final product.

being shot with a stationary camera or a moving one, but frankly, I'd rather get caught up in the presentation itself than think about where I'm being filmed from. I say let the cameraman and his post-production team do the work to make the shoot look as alive as possible. That's their job.

However, if you're making and producing your own video, just be sure that it's shot with sufficient light—that there aren't any shadows—and that the sound quality is better than good. You don't need to make it fancy; you just need to make sure that your lighting and sound won't distract the audience from your message.

MAKE EYE CONTACT

Remember that while body language and vocals do come into play on camera, your gaze is the most important physical element to focus on. Look at that camera like you're looking at a person—like you care—and communicate all the emotion you can. Just as you would if you were standing in front of a live audience, incorporate the 5 C's of a commanding speaker—be caring, confident, comfortable, credible, and charismatic—and the camera will love you.

THE BOTTOM LINE

If you train yourself to see the camera as a person, and if you do the exercises I suggest in this chapter, you will increase the impact of your on-camera presence—your personality will come shining through, and your audience will get to experience not only your words and your message, but the real you.

CHAPTER 26

Creating an "Impact" Presentation

LET'S EXAMINE THE INGREDIENTS of an "impact" presentation and the methods a speaker can use so that, at the end of their speech, the audience is thinking, *Wow!* or, *My goodness, I had no idea* or, *All right, let's get this thing done!* or, *I'm upset about this, and I want to take some action.*

The reactions I've just described will occur when the content and delivery of a presentation are exciting and moving—in other words, when the experience creates an impact. A definition of "impact" could be "a significant, marked effect on an audience, or individuals in an audience, that leads them to be **inspired** to do something." This "inspiration" could take the form of members of the audience making a decision, taking positive action, getting out of the trap they were in and moving forward, or changing the course of things that weren't going well for them.

USE STRONG SUPPORT SOURCES

When you consider some of the ingredients of an impact presentation, I always use examples that directly relate to the point I'm making, and I incorporate support sources (in order to build credibility), because it makes the case for why my audience should believe what I'm saying. *Proving that what you're saying is true* adds to the impact of your speech.

IMPINGE UPON YOUR AUDIENCE

To **impinge** means to really drive a point home, to hit the mark and strike a nerve. In public speaking, this can be achieved through visuals, sound, evocative examples, or a combination of the three. Together, these elements can have a significant impact upon your audience.

Accumulations of impingement, throughout a presentation, really cause a dramatic effect among your audience. When your audience feels, hears, and sees what you're describing—when it impacts them emotionally—they are more likely to be moved to action.

One way to make an impingement during your presentation is by creating an illustration of something through an actual demonstration. During seminars and workshops, for example, I often bring someone up onstage from the audience to show them some coaching tips and take them through a revealing, evolving, changing process in as little as fifteen minutes. This live demonstration makes a significant difference not only for the person being coached but for the audience as well, because it takes what I'm talking about out of the theoretical and makes it into something tangible.

SCHINDLER'S LIST AS AN EXAMPLE OF SUCCESSFUL IMPINGEMENT

Steven Spielberg's *Schindler's List* is perhaps one of the most successful examples I can think of when it comes to intentional audience impingement. Each scene builds upon the previous one, offering a searing depiction of the evil acts that actually took place during this horrific time period. From the forced eviction of people from their homes to the fatal shooting of innocent camp prisoners, the viewer is impinged upon scene after scene—and the film culminates with considerable emotional impact as it leads viewers to contemplate that this brand of evil still exists in the world and is taking on a new form of terrorism.

In presenting, a speaker who creates a series of impinging impressions will unavoidably create an emotional impact upon their audience that will stay with the audience long after the presentation is over. These impingements certainly do not have to be draining or upsetting, however—any emotion designed to move an audience will work. Perhaps you wish to move your audience to stand up and take action, or simply to experience the pure joy of inspiration—either way, as long as you create continuous impingements, you will end up with an impact presentation.

As a speaker, you will strike a chord with an audience when you make yourself involved. Your demeanor and your ability to immerse yourself in the attitude or emotion of the message you are delivering can make all the difference—whether your message is heartwarming or heart-wrenching, it's the way in which you express it and send it out to your audience that matters. It is a combination of appropriate emotion and powerful messaging that leads to impact.

OTHER TOOLS FOR MAKING AN IMPACT

Transitions are a great tool you can use to bring about impact. These can be questions to the audience ("Are you following me?" "Would you like to know what I did next?"), or they can be more subtle, physical movements (moving forward to introduce a point and then moving back when you're progressing to the next one). (See chapter 6, "Using Transitions to Keep Your Audience Interested," for more details on this.)

Another way to make an impact is by getting your audience looking at things. Invade their privacy; get their attention. That's why you're there, after all. Put something right in front of them and let it hit home. Then observe their reactions. Even if they don't look emotional, they're feeling it inside. I've had people upon whom I didn't think I'd had any effect on come up to me after a presentation and tell me how moved they were. You never know!

THE BOTTOM LINE

The true value of your presentation lies in what happens after it's over. If audience members reach out to you afterward and want more—if they want to email you, purchase your book, attend more of your events, or subscribe on your website—*then* you know you have achieved the product of your presentation.

If you use impingement throughout your presentation—if you properly utilize the tools at your disposal, driving home every point you make as well as you can—your audience will be open to the impact you wish to make. When you prime your audience in this way, getting them to respond to your call to action will be a no-brainer, because you will have already laid out all the ingredients to have them follow you. Given the right groundwork, your audience will walk away from your presentation moved and ready to act.

EXERCISE #21: CREATE IMPINGING STATEMENTS

Create several impinging (nerve-hitting) statements for your audience that you think will effectively drive home a point about your message or call to action.

Practice with an audience. Note any emotional impact these statements might have on them.

KEY FACTORS OF AN
IMPACT PRESENTATION

- Give very real examples of the points you make, preferably ones that the audience has their own experiences with (knowing your audience is key here).

- Be as descriptive as possible in your storytelling—draw your audience in.

- Outwardly express emotion to your audience to support your message.

- Use physical movements to drive your point home.

- Pause or slow down when you make major, emotional points, to allow them to sink in for your audience.

- Use emotionally evocative visuals to illustrate your points.

- Demonstrate a "before and after" change to the audience, when possible—this kind of tool impacts the audience and also injects instant credibility into your presentation.

CHAPTER 27

Motivating Your Audience to Accept Your Help

LET'S LOOK AT A SIMPLE and effective sequence of items in a scale I call the "Problem—Solution Scale," which I have trained speakers to use to move an audience to commit to any call to action—whether it's a product, a service, an idea, or any other intended audience end result.

At its core, isn't sales really just creating opportunities to help others? To give or provide people with what they need or want? Approach your presentation with this mindset: you are there to move your audience to accept your help in accessing an idea, a product, or a service that will benefit them in some way.

RECOGNIZING THE PROBLEM

The first thing any good presentation does is help the audience recognize what the problem they're facing is. Let's say it's deteriorating health and you want to offer them a package of specialized, organic nutritional supplements designed to help them improve their health. Well, first you have to make them aware that they need to improve their health. You might, for example, offer some evidence that supports the idea that we are all less healthy today because of the biochemical additives in our food and water and other factors. Do what you need to do to get your audience to recognize the problem you're offering a solution to.

EXPERIENCING THE PAIN OF THE PROBLEM

Next, paint a picture of the *pain* the problem creates. This is a universal sales tool: getting your subject to really feel what you're talking about. If your audience can't feel the pain—if they don't understand how it directly affects them—it won't matter what you're offering. So describe the aftereffects of bad nutrition or unhealthy practices; describe what it feels like to live with physical pain or inconsistent sleep; describe how difficult it is to feel constantly irritated with your family and coworkers. Whatever personal issues the problem might create, make your audience experience them as fully as possible.

RECOGNIZING THE CONSEQUENCES OF NO ACTION TAKEN

Next, what if you did nothing? What if you made no effort to solve the problem? Make sure your audience recognizes that not only will the problem not go away, it will get *worse*—and describe the consequences in detail. For example: "Are you willing to live with a toxic body that will lessen your chances of longevity and enjoying your later years? Do you really want to risk allowing this issue to stifle your work and creativity, or even your sex life?" It is important to impinge here so that your audience recognizes the ripple effect of not taking any action.

RECOGNIZING THE CONSEQUENCES OF TAKING ACTION

Now that your listeners understand what will happen if they don't do anything to counteract their problem, explain what will happen if they *do* take action. What will happen if they stay away from toxic foods, get off those pain medications, eat more healthfully, exercise, and follow a program designed to help them maintain it? What will the ripple effects be then? Get them to see the consequences of doing something that will reduce or eliminate the pain and negativity associated with their problem.

DECIDING IMPROVEMENT OR CHANGE IS NECESSARY

Once you've gotten your audience to recognize how much better things would be if they took action about their problem, it shouldn't take much more effort to convince them that change or improvement is the way to go. Here is where you introduce your solution to the problem they suffer from, to educate your audience about all the benefits associated with it and to demonstrate why it works.

THE PROBLEM—SOLUTION SCALE

Reaching for
the Solution

Deciding Improvement or
Change Is Necessary

Recognizing the Consequences of
Taking Action

Recognizing the Consequences of
No Action Taken

Experiencing the Pain of
the Problem

Recognizing the Problem

REACHING FOR THE SOLUTION

Applying this scale will help you move your audience to take the positive action you know is helpful for them. Before you began your presentation, most of the people in your audience were probably not open to accepting your solution or help—but now that you've moved them through these five steps, they should be receptive to your message.

THE BOTTOM LINE

When you stand before an audience to give a presentation, you become a leader—and it is a leader's responsibility and duty to move their audiences, work teams, communities, and constituents to aspire for more. You are not simply giving a speech; you are inspiring your listeners to take positive action and achieve worthwhile, productive results in the world. The Problem—Solution Scale offers a simple, step-by-step approach to doing just that.

A PRACTICAL EXERCISE

Employing the Problem—Solution Scale, construct a sixty-second commercial about your product or service. See if you can move your audience or viewer from recognizing the problem to opening up to the solution in this short span of time. Don't forget to use benefit statements to enlighten them about the many benefits of your solution!

EXERCISE #22: CREATE YOUR OWN PROBLEM—SOLUTION FORMULA

Write out your own Problem—Solution formula for your speech using suitable examples, including benefit statements. Make sure you present the problem, pain, consequence, decision, and solution to your audience in sequence, moving them through each step until they are ready to accept your solution.

CHAPTER 28

Emotion and Your Call to Action

EVOKING EMOTION IS A standard technique used in sales training because people need to see and feel emotion before they'll buy the product or service someone is selling. Note that it's no coincidence that the word "emotion" actually contains "motion"—it's the means by which people are moved.

WILL IT MOVE THEM?

When giving a speech, the question you must ask yourself is "Will it stir or incite my audience?" If the answer is yes, then there is emotion in your presentation.

When a singer performs, they must outwardly express their emotions to an audience in order for that audience to truly *feel* the lyrics of their song. When that happens, the audience is *moved and affected* by their performance. The same is true of a dynamic speaker who is committed to getting their point across. Any emotion (fear, grief, anger, joy, excitement) can be used to wake people out of their solemn state of ho-hum lethargy—and as long as it relates to your message, it will be a welcome addition to your presentation.

TAKE YOUR AUDIENCE'S EMOTIONAL PULSE

As we discussed in chapter 1, human beings have two main motivators: resisting pain and attaining pleasure. Offering people *freedom from something* concentrates on prevention and motivates them with examples of how to avoid pain. Offering people the opportunity to *seek or achieve something* stimulates their creativity and motivates them with the promise of pleasure.

When you know your audience's emotional pulse, you can determine how best to approach them, as well as which examples and supports are most appropriate to use. For instance, if you are an investment strategist, it's important to know whether the members of your audience are more concerned with *saving* their money or *growing* it.

Again, gathering information about your audience is crucial. Taking a survey before your presentation is an effective approach; so is asking the audience questions as you are presenting, to get their feedback. (This second tactic may be more difficult, though, because you have to stay focused on your topic even as you keep track of the answers to the questions that you are putting out and switching gears based upon the information you're receiving.)

THE BOTTOM LINE

However you decide to obtain your information, you should always adapt your performance to the audience you're presenting to. Emotion is a key ingredient by which an audience is spurred on to a call to action, so you need to be able to identify and evoke the appropriate emotions for your particular audience.

EXERCISE #23: BRAINSTORM POSITIVE AND NEGATIVE EMOTIONAL FACTORS

Come up with several examples of both positive and negative emotional factors that could motivate your audience to the call to action you have prepared for them.

EMOTIONAL FACTORS THAT MOTIVATE AN AUDIENCE

This chart shows a breakdown of positive versus negative emotions. Your audience is either motivated to attain pleasure or motivated to resist pain, and these are key indicators that a speaker can use to identify the character of the audience they're addressing. Knowing what kind of audience you're talking to will help you tailor your speech to a language or phraseology that will attract the most favorable response. Keep in mind that many audiences contain a mix of people from both sides of the emotional chart; in those cases, your benefit statements should include information that targets both types of motivations.

EMOTIONALLY POSITIVE AUDIENCES are motivated through	EMOTIONALLY NEGATIVE AUDIENCES are motivated through
Achieving pleasure	Resisting pain
Building the future	Maintaining the status quo
Freedom to achieve	Freedom from failure
Creating	Preventing

CHAPTER 29

Thirty No Fear Speaking Tips

THE FOLLOWING THIRTY TIPS serve as a distillation of the key lessons you've learned in the course of this book. Feel free to review them anytime you have an upcoming speech or presentation, and to use them as a reference guide. As long as you keep these tips and guidelines in mind, you'll have no trouble living up to your role as a No Fear Speaker.

1. Unscripted and conversational delivery naturally attracts.

2. Look, don't think! Observe everything and everyone.

3. Don't memorize, recognize!

4. Create correct content for your own introduction, and prepare your introducer.

5. Know your audience and their interests, needs, and wants.

6. Write down a concise summary of your presentation objective, purpose, outcome, or call to action.

7. Construct your framework (outline) before filling in the details.

8. Design an attention-getting opening.

9. Build your credibility by gathering detailed support for your key points.

10. Craft a climactic, compelling, and memorable conclusion.

11. Use transitions to make your points connect well and flow smoothly.

12. Never end a presentation with a Q&A period.

13. Less is more. Edit your presentation.

14. PowerPoint slides are visual aids, not the core of your presentation, and they are most effective when they contain minimal copy.

15. An inspiring story from your personal experience creates impact, raises trust, and imbues your presentation with humor.

16. You will enhance your audience reach if you utilize benefit statements throughout your presentation.

17. Varying voice, body movement, pace, and attitude dissolves monotony.

18. Engaging the audience to interact creates more involvement and positive impact.

19. A Q&A period should be used to support and fortify your call to action.

20. Outwardly express appropriate emotion and physicality to move your audience to take action.

21. Get your audience to contemplate the consequences of doing nothing versus taking action.

22. Evaluate your audience based on the two basic motivations: achieving pleasure and resisting pain.

23. Observe your audience and listen attentively to them during your presentation—that's the mark of a great speaker.

24. Adopting a martial arts mentality and resisting nothing will always solve the problem of a difficult audience.

25. Practice your speech in front of a person or a camera but never in front of a mirror, as speaking to yourself is introverting.

26. Always keep in mind the three key connections when practicing or delivering your speech live: 1) speaker connected to message; 2) speaker connected to audience; 3) message connected to audience.

27. Continually impinging on your audience is crucial for an "impact" presentation.

28. Cultivating a comfortable on-camera presence depends on recognizing the distance between you and the camera.

29. Create a logistics checklist prior to your speech to ensure all necessities are in place and backups are available.

30. Never give a presentation or deliver to an audience you have little or no interest in. Integrity is your beacon!

End of Part III: Practical

UTILIZING ALL OF THE OUTLINING and preparation steps you've learned in the course of this book, prepare, organize, and deliver a fifteen- to twenty-minute impact presentation. Record it and play it back, then rerecord it and play it for yourself again until you achieve an authentic delivery that connects to your audience and successfully communicates your call to action.

Special Offer: Contact our No Fear Speaking Headquarters Training Facility at (727) 489-2349 or info@nofearspeaking.com to have your Final Practical critiqued at no cost.

My Call to Action for You

I HAVE WRITTEN THIS BOOK because the special and unique ideas that you possess need an advocate—they need to be passionately articulated before other people. I want you to be inspired to speak, and I want the people whom you speak to in turn to be inspired by you. I want you to know that you can stand up before others—before your peers in business, before your entire community—and you can make a difference in their lives.

You have read what I've written because you want to give wings to your words—because you want to move others with your thoughts and your convictions. This book has provided you with the map to do just that.

So, learn the fundamentals. Absorb the knowledge necessary for you to effortlessly express yourself. Then, once you know what you need to do, practice, practice, practice.

Life is an art. One of my favorite expressions is this: If you scratch the essence of a person, you'll get an artist. In other words, if you get down to a person's core, their genuine self, you'll find an artist residing there. What's so great about being an artist? Above all, they *create*—and to create is nothing less than miraculous. But the greatest of artists, in my opinion, is not the artist who works in stone or paint or sound or movement, but rather one who works with life itself. The product that such an artist delivers to the world is their own life, fully lived, every second of every day. That is what I fervently wish for you: that you will become the great artist of your own life by manifesting, to all around you, your most deeply held aspirations.

I thank you for having taken this journey with me. I know from personal experience that the wisdom in this book has the power to intensely and infinitely change your life for the better. But nobody becomes a master in a day, a week, a month, or even a year. It takes unrelenting perseverance and commitment to one's goals and ideals to truly succeed. Can you make such a commitment to your own success? Are you willing to do whatever it takes to achieve your greatest aspirations?

The greatest failure in life, in my opinion, is not the failure to obtain one's deepest desire but the failure to dream—because it is only in dreaming that one is motivated to act and make their goals a reality. When you dream, you can no longer rest comfortably on a sofa of excuses and say, "I never knew what I wanted" or, "I was never sure of anything" or, "Nothing ever really made much of a difference in my life."

What is life if not the utter exhilaration of a great challenge or pitting yourself against the limiting thoughts that have enclosed you, suffocated you, and kept you from running on all cylinders? What is it if not that private moment of victory when you know that you have triumphed against all odds and have scaled heights you never thought possible?

I call on you now to dream—to dream bigger than you have ever dared.

I urge you to dare to become great.

You were born for it.

Just as the mighty oak lies inside the tiny seed, your greatness lies inside you.

Maybe you once believed you were a sheep because you lost your way, or because others were too blinded by their own failings to see the real you. But, I tell you that if you look deep into the pool and look for who you truly are, you will not see a sheep gazing back at you; you will see a lion.

There is no time like the present, so take action. Take the tools I'm offering you, and continue on the road to greatness. Embrace the destiny that is meant for you and you alone.

Your Inspiration

MY FAVORITE SPEECH OF ALL time is from the film The Great Dictator, starring the great Charlie Chaplin. It is his most impressive acting feat.

This highly acclaimed speech, which takes place at the end of the movie, is the most impactful, emotion-evoking, searing satire on evil I have ever seen. It is dramatic, relevant, beautifully delivered, and totally inspiring. Even more amazing is the fact that Charlie Chaplin was the one to deliver it so masterfully, given that he made his name as a silent actor. I consider this the most important speech in recorded history, and I highly recommend that you look it up and watch it. When you see it, you will understand why.

I have had the good fortune of experiencing many inspiring speeches: formal and informal presentations from great world leaders, famous celebrities, renowned artists, and distinguished educators, yes, but also from unknown high school teachers, church pastors, and family members. What I've learned throughout the years is that anyone can inspire others to aspire for more—to embark on the journey toward their life's purpose.

Do not underestimate or shortchange the depth or richness of your experiences. You carry with you a bounty of ability, skill, knowledge, and creativity that, if you access it, can inspire others. Every life yearning to succeed and exceed results in valuable life lessons—and these are the lessons your audiences show up to learn.

But in addition to your own life experiences, there is much content already in existence that we can use in our speeches to inspire our audiences to be more, do more, and achieve more. The hallmark of a great speaker is the ability to use every tool at their disposal to wake up their audience, transform their perspective, and rally them to action—whether those tools are of their own making or are the products of those who have preceded them.

Over my many years of public speaking, I have delivered my own "notable quotables"—wise words from great thinkers and leaders across history—in a number of my presentations, to drive my points home and inspire my audience. Below, I have gathered together a handful of these quotes for your own reference and divided them into six categories: Integrity, Competence, Confidence, Communication, Courage, and Leadership. These are highly desirable qualities that many people strive to achieve, and they are the qualities I feel speakers can best lean upon to enthuse their audiences and move them to greater levels of achievement and virtue. Take a look, and see what you think.

INTEGRITY

"Your time is limited, so don't waste it living someone else's life. Don't be trapped by dogma, which is living with the results of other people's thinking. Don't let the noise of others' opinions drown your own inner voice. And most important, have the courage to follow your heart and intuition. They somehow already know what you truly want to become. Everything else is secondary."

—Steve Jobs

"I don't believe in a fate that will fall on us no matter what we do. I do believe in a fate that will fall on us if we do nothing."

—Ronald Reagan

"There is only one way to avoid criticism: do nothing, say nothing, and be nothing."

—Aristotle

"If you want to know what a man's like, take a good look at how he treats his inferiors, not his equals."

—J. K. Rowling, *Harry Potter and the Goblet of Fire*

"Somebody once said that in looking for people to hire, you look for three qualities: integrity, intelligence, and energy. And if you don't have the first, the other two will kill you. You think about it; it's true. If you hire somebody without [integrity], you really want them to be dumb and lazy."

—Warren Buffett

"No one can make you feel inferior without your consent."

—Eleanor Roosevelt

COMPETENCE

"It's not the load that breaks you down, it's the way you carry it."

—Lou Holtz

"If money is your hope for independence, you will never have it. The only real security that a man will have in this world is a reserve of knowledge, experience, and ability."

—Henry Ford

"The way to get started is to quit talking and begin doing."

—Walt Disney

"Education costs money. But then so does ignorance."

—Sir Claus Moser

"I have been impressed with the urgency of doing. Knowing is not enough; we must apply. Being willing is not enough; we must do."

—Leonardo da Vinci

CONFIDENCE

"Success consists of going from failure to failure without loss of enthusiasm."

—Winston Churchill

"The circulation of confidence is better than the circulation of money."

—James Madison

"I didn't fail the test. I just found 100 ways to do it wrong."

—Benjamin Franklin

"Nothing in the world can take the place of persistence. Talent will not; nothing is more common than unsuccessful men with talent. Genius will not; unrewarded genius is almost a proverb. Education will not; the world is full of educated derelicts. Persistence and determination alone are omnipotent. The slogan 'press on' has solved and always will solve the problems of the human race."

—Calvin Coolidge

"You miss 100 percent of the shots you don't take."

—Wayne Gretzky

COMMUNICATION

"Every child is an artist. The problem is how to remain an artist once he grows up."

—Pablo Picasso

"The greatest gift you can give someone is your own personal development. I used to say, 'If you will take care of me, I will take care of you.' Now I say, 'I will take care of me for you if you will take care of you for me.'"

—Jim Rohn

"You never lose by loving. You always lose by holding back."

—Barbara De Angelis

"Either write something worth reading or do something worth writing."

—Benjamin Franklin

"I'm a great believer that any tool that enhances communication has profound effects in terms of how people can learn from each other, and how they can achieve the kind of freedoms that they're interested in."

—Bill Gates

COURAGE

"I've missed more than nine thousand shots in my career. I've lost almost three hundred games. Twenty-six times I've been trusted to take the game-winning shot and missed. I've failed over and over and over again in my life. And that is why I succeed."

—Michael Jordan

"In spite of everything I still believe that people are really good at heart. I simply can't build up my hopes on a foundation consisting of confusion, misery, and death."

—Anne Frank

"Life is 10 percent what happens to you and 90 percent how you respond to it."

—Lou Holtz

"The best revenge is massive success."

—Frank Sinatra

"If you hear a voice within you say 'you cannot paint,' then by all means paint, and that voice will be silenced."

—Vincent van Gogh

"When everything seems to be going against you, remember that the airplane takes off against the wind, not with it."

—Henry Ford

LEADERSHIP

"Leadership is not magnetic personality—that can just as well be a glib tongue. It is not 'making friends and influencing people'—that is flattery. Leadership is lifting a person's vision to higher sights, the raising of a person's performance to a higher standard, the building of a personality beyond its normal limitations."

—Peter F. Drucker

"Here's to the crazy ones. The misfits. The rebels. The troublemakers. The round pegs in the square holes. The ones who see things differently. They're not fond of rules. . . . You can quote them, disagree with them, glorify or vilify them. About the only thing you can't do is ignore them. Because they change things. They push the human race forward. And while some may see them as the crazy ones, we see genius. Because the people who are crazy enough to think they can change the world are the ones who do."

—Steve Jobs

"Be a yardstick of quality. Some people aren't used to an environment where excellence is expected."

—Steve Jobs

"There is no such thing as society. There are individual men and women, and there are families."

—Margaret Thatcher

"It is my daily mood that makes the weather. I possess tremendous power to make life miserable or joyous. I can be a tool of torture or an instrument of inspiration. I can humiliate or humor, hurt or heal. In all situations, it is my response that decides whether a crisis is escalated or de-escalated, and a person is humanized or de-humanized. If we treat people as they are, we make them worse. If we treat people as they ought to be, we help them become what they are capable of becoming."

—Johann Wolfgang Goethe

"This is the true joy in life, the being used for a purpose recognized by yourself as a mighty one; the being a force of nature instead of a feverish, selfish little clod of ailments and grievances complaining that the world will not devote itself to making you happy. I am of the opinion that my life belongs to the whole community, and as long as I live it is my privilege to do for it whatever I can. I want to be thoroughly used up when I die, for the harder I work the more I live. I rejoice in life for its own sake. Life is no 'brief candle' for me. It is a sort of splendid torch which I have got hold of for the moment, and I want to make it burn as brightly as possible before handing it on to future generations."

—George Bernard Shaw

These quotes inspire me, but what about you? What inspires you? What in life has had a major, positive impact on you, has made you feel and think more clearly, has motivated you to try and given you the courage to press on? What major life experiences have you lived through that have caused you to summon up more truth, more insight, and more drive to achieve?

These are your inspirations. These are the real and true ideals, principles, and passions that make great speakers. They will inspire audiences because you believe in them—because they are genuine.

You have your inspirations. Now use them, express them, move your audience with them. Embrace them, and let them help you deliver speeches that will change the people who hear them.

Next Action Steps

UP YOUR GAME AND ACCELERATE YOUR SUCCESS!
These simple, easy to use additional *No Fear Speaking* tools are available at www.nofearspeaking.com.

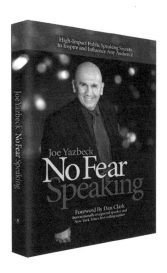

Scan this QR Code to purchase paperback, hard cover, and all other materials at NoFearSpeaking.com.

NO FEAR SPEAKING QUICK REFERENCE GUIDE

A Reference Guide of *No Fear Speaking* Illustrations in Hard Copy Spiral Bound Format.

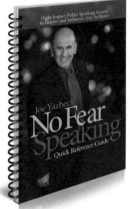

A complete collection of all the charts, tables, tips and illustrations compiled from the book, *No Fear Speaking* in one simple to use reference guide. If you are looking to organize a speech and want summary illustrations for quick preparation, this is what you are looking for! An easy to search summary of all the key elements of presentation tools condensed together in one reference guide.

NO FEAR SPEAKING AUDIO BOOK PROGRAM

This captivating 3-hour and 20-minute audio book program

is actually narrated by the master speaker and coach himself, Joe Yazbeck, and includes a professional announcer for each chapter and practical exercise as well as compelling music introducing and ending each chapter. You will receive each chapter as an individual file for convenient future brush up re-study.

The **NO FEAR SPEAKING** ONLINE VIDEO TRAINING SYSTEMS FOR SPEAKER CERTIFICATION.

ONLINE VIDEO TRAINING
FOR SPEAKER CERTIFICATION
CORPORATE

Both Academic and Corporate Training Editions Available!

ONLINE VIDEO TRAINING
FOR SPEAKER CERTIFICATION
ACADEMIC

This online video training program comes in 3 packages to choose from and includes:

- **No Fear Speaking Core Curriculum**
  (includes 26 Video Training Segments on Speech Design, Speaker Magnetism & Moving Your Audience)

- **No Fear Speaking Business/Executive Communications**
  (includes 5 Video training Segments on Speaker Tools for Getting Hired, Successful Sales Presentations, Speaking Skills for Great Networking & Managing Effective Meetings)

- **No Fear Speaking E Book**

- **No Fear Speaking Quick Reference Guide**

- **Subscription to The Speakers Voice**

Some packages include:

- Public Speaking Coaching session by Joe Yazbeck

- Income and Lead Generator Session for Speakers

- In-Depth Critique of your Next Presentation or Speech

Book Joe Yazbeck for speaking engagements anywhere in the world. Call: (727) 489-2349 or (727) 741-1029 or email: info@nofearspeaking.com

Further Study

GO TO WWW.NOFEARSPEAKING.COM TO:

1. Register for No Fear Speaking seminars, workshops, online video training courses, webinars, and introductory events.

2. Discover how to become a No Fear Speaking trainer/ coach.

3. Book Joe Yazbeck for speaking engagements any- where in the world or call (727) 489-2349 or (727) 741-1029 or email info@nofearspeaking.com.

GO TO WWW.PRESTIGELEADER.COM TO:

Find out more about the following successful corporate training programs at Prestige Leadership Advisors or by emailing info@prestigeleader.com.

LEADERSHIP & EXECUTIVE ACHIEVEMENT SKILLS

Tools of Inspirational Leadership, Delegation Skills, Strategic Planning, Policy & Procedures, Executive Communications, Team Target Attainment, and Essentials of Gamesmanship

INCREASING BUSINESS PRODUCTIVITY & EFFICIENCY

Time Management, Production Planning, Problem Solving, and Team Coordination

RAISING EMPLOYEE PERFORMANCE LEVELS

Employee Training Programs, Training the Trainer, and Quality Control Tools

HOW TO BUILD AN ETHICAL, COMPETENT & PRODUCTIVE TEAM

Accountability Training and Creating Future Company Leaders

EFFECTIVE EMPLOYEE/MANAGEMENT COMMUNICATIONS

Communications Training (includes employees and their managers/supervisors)

GROUP PROSPECTING: MOTIVATING AUDIENCES TO BUY

Sales Presentation Training

DYNAMIC PUBLIC SPEAKING & EFFECTIVE PRESENTATION

Preparing, organizing, and delivering an impact presentation or speech to any live audience or through media channels for any purpose and any size audience

WORKABLE TOOLS TO MASTER THE ART OF NEGOTIATION

How to get a win-win result out of any negotiation process

STRATEGIC PLANNING: VITAL STEPS TO GUARANTEE FUTURE EXPANSION

The essential steps to carrying a company from its current scene to its ideal standard

SUCCESSFUL HIRING & TRAINING OF PERSONNEL

Vital elements of the hiring process; converting qualified candidates into new personnel, and the proper training programs for supporting their success

SALES & MARKETING SOLUTIONS TO INCREASE BOTTOM LINE

Prospecting and sales skills training to increase new, qualified prospects and clients.

Acknowledgments

Norm Thalheimer, whose brilliant literary mind greatly assisted me with the shaping of *No Fear Speaking.* You are a true friend and just plain priceless.

Carl Wagner, whose guidance and direction as my college dramatic arts mentor inspired me to understand not only the value of expressing oneself in the world but also how to use the creative process in mentoring others to give great performances.

Margie Rosenstein of NuEdge Designs whose exquisite creative design talent helped visually define my work.

Gretchen Cain Wells, whose published articles on my work helped accelerate the creation of my book.

Brooke Warner and her team, for their expertise, guidance, and direction on this book. Thank you for your patience, understanding, and professionalism.

Chris Paradies of Paradies Law for his astute legal guidance and, more importantly, his unconditional friendship.

Chris Gibson of AccuSource Media, **Howard VanEs** of Let's Write Books, Inc., and **Ginger Marks** of DocUmeant Publishing & Designs for their marketing and publishing support.

IN MEMORIAM

John Lenberg, whose mark on the world made it such a better place before and after he left it. You are a prime example of how to live a remarkably full life. We remain Brothers of the Heart.

Tom Morgan, whose influence as a speaker, teacher, artist, and humanitarian made a profound difference in my life and inspired me to pave sturdy roads to positively impact others.

About the Author

JOE YAZBECK IS THE FOUNDER, president, and CEO of Prestige Leadership Advisors. His mission is to facilitate leaders in becoming dynamic, powerful communicators so that they can significantly influence the world around them. Having worked with heads of state, leaders of major corporations, high-ranking military officers, political candidates, and best-selling authors, Joe Yazbeck is a highly sought-after leadership and communications coach. Government and business leaders around the globe seek his counsel and his company's services with handling PR and strategic direction, media training for launching a new brand, influencing board members, speaking to government committees, winning a political campaign, creating a successful exit strategy or recovering from a loss of confidence, etc.

To complement the services of Prestige Leadership Advisors, Joe created the No Fear Speaking System which offers a host of communications services, including executive-level speaker training, negotiation skills, media presentations for radio and TV, sales presentations, courtroom/trial presentations, etc. Joe has also authored a companion book by the same title, "No Fear Speaking: High Impact Presentation Skills and Public Speaking Secrets to Inspire and Influence Any Audience," which is an Amazon bestseller. DVDs, videos, online trainings, and other support materials are also available.

Joe's newest venture, "Leaders Taking Action," is an elite group of leaders from diverse industries and countries formed as a coalition whose sole purpose is to help resolve many of the world's most pressing problems. Contact us at info@prestigeleader.com to learn more about this organization, its strategy, and requirements for participation.

Consistent with his values and responsibilities for social change, Joe serves as chairman of the board for the Community Learning Center, an award-winning organization that provides professional tutors to young kids and adults and with the goal of eradicating illiteracy. Joe continues to serve as an active member of Citizens Commission on Human Rights and The Way to Happiness Foundation. He is also the co-founder of Veterans Transition Academy, which helps returning veterans build a career and transition to civilian life.

Visit his websites at:

www.PrestigeLeader.com and www.NoFearSpeaking.com